THE PURPOSE OF SINGLENESS

The Purpose of Singleness
Published by Casting Seeds Publishing

Scripture quotations unless otherwise indicated are from the ESV ® Bible (The Holy Bible, English Standard Version), Copyright © 2001 by Crossway. Used by permission. All rights reserved.

Published in the United States by Casting Seeds Publishing an extension and aid to UNPLUGGED.

***

Websites and Social Media sites:
Website: IAMUNPLUGGED.COM | MYCOACHJOSH.ORG
Books: UNPLUGGED & WorldWarM3 | Amazon.com Search: Joshua Eze
Social Media: **@MYCOACHJOSH**

COACH JOSH

ARE YOU WHOLE?

Table of Contents

Epilogue: *Words from the Coach*

Most if not all of us have a desire for companionship. This is nothing new – God addressed it early in Genesis with Adam and Eve, when He said, "It is not good for man to be alone." However, there is a purpose to singleness and that is what this book is about. Solomon listed some of the different seasons of life in Ecclesiastes and singleness is a season as well. The purpose of any season is to glorify God. This book will address this season and how to navigate through it and seek God's face in the process. Without God we would be like fish out of water. The Bible says that in Him we live, move, and have our being. He is the essence of our lives and He alone determines our worth and dignity; it is sad that His creation is indifferent about getting to know Him. God deserves all of the glory in our lives no matter what stage or season of life we are in. Every tangible and intangible gift was given to us by God, whether you are an artist, businessman, or are in ministry.

The moment that humanity walked away from God, our gifts ceased to have any value. This changed with God's plan to redeem mankind through Christ. Our gifts are no longer for our glory but are to be used for the Great Commission. He desires for each of us to maximize our potential and focus on staying in His presence until he takes us to the next stage, whether it be singleness or the career we've been hoping for. We have to understand that life is comprised of stages and seasons. We have to learn to be content in each stage before God takes us to the next stage. Each stage prepares us for the next one. This book deals specifically with the importance of being whole before entering into a relationship or marriage. It will help you with your personal development overall and can be applied to other areas of your life, not just relationships and marriage. The purpose of your life is to glorify God – not to seek after a spouse or career. The will of God will naturally address all of these but you must seek Him first before these things. My heart is for you to seek His heart and not His hand; to love Him like you never have before and to treasure Him above everything and anyone else. I hope this book helps you grow into the best version of yourself that you can be. – **Coach**

Do Me a Favor

I believe this book is going to impact a lot of lives and I need your help to do so. If you feel like this book will be beneficial to your friends, family, co-workers etc. please share where they can find a copy of this book and let's help them discover their worth and their purpose. Feel free to a start small group and feel free to share quotes from this book or pictures online utilizing the # tag #ThePurposeOfSingleness or #MyCoachJosh. I look forward to connecting with you online and I pray that you enjoy my 3rd book *The Purpose of Singleness*.

1

Chapter 1: *There is a Purpose for Everything*

God holds the definition of everything. Every single thing that He created under the sun, he first defined. This book deals specifically with His definitions of singleness, marriage, sex, and love and what happens when these definitions aren't followed.

One issue in our culture is that many people have allowed themselves to be defined by everything but God. The world's system is designed by Satan to derail us from the original definitions of singleness, marriage, sex, love, and life. He knows that if he can steer believers away from God's original design for these, that they will become perverted in the way they think about them. Perversion is the opposite of God's original intent for something. Look at our world today. How many people at this moment aren't embracing their singleness? How many people are prematurely pursuing marriage? How many people have become infatuated and mistaken it for love? God does everything in order. My question to you is this: is your life in order or is it stagnant? Are you spinning your wheels and not going anywhere? Are you waiting for God to "promote" you to something better? Promotion only comes through doing things in the correct order. You have to ask yourself right now if you are doing whatever it takes to be whole, whether you are single or married. God does not budge based upon how many tears are cried or how much we beg. He moves the moment He sees that we are prepared for the next level. He holds the definition of life not just for humanity in general, but for you specifically. He has already defined your life. God is not bound by time – He is an eternal God and right now He knows your past, present, and future. He already knows the whole spectrum of your life. He has predestined you and called you for a time such as this. However, in order for you to align yourself with His will you have to have your life in order.

Skipping Steps

God has laid out the blueprint for your life and it involves taking certain steps. These are steps to ensure that you grow and mature. What we often fail to realize is that each step is important and when we rush through these steps it is dangerous. Satan loves it when we rush, because when we rush we "Ruin, Uproot, Shift, and Hinder" our growth and development. We need to remember that we are programmed to be impulsive and impatient. This system is designed for us to be discontent with the step we are on and rush ahead to the next stage. ALL steps matter. God desires for you to live your life under an umbrella of patience. He knows that in order for you to be whom he purposed you to be, you have to be guided by patience. Think of a child and the necessary steps that must be taken in order for him or her to grow. Before they can run, they must walk; before they can walk, they must crawl. Imagine if they never learned to crawl – they wouldn't have the ability to play sports or do the normal things that other children can. They cannot skip the crawling stage – it is essential. Everything in life is predicated on the step or stage before it. You cannot get to steps 10, 11, or 12, until you complete steps one through nine. God has a purpose for you in this exact moment and His timing is perfect. He holds the definition of everything – have you checked His dictionary lately? Have you sought His face to find out who you are? If you want to be promoted and get to the next stage, you have to understand how God works. His ways are not our ways and His thoughts are not our thoughts. He does everything in order. This does not mean that you have to be perfect for Him to promote you – you just have to be aware of His purposes for you and follow His perfect order. You have to ask yourself if your soul, mind, and body are healthy. Have you allowed yourself to be washed with His word? Have you allowed yourself to get to know Him? Have you let go of any hidden sins? Is there perversion in your life?

Self-examination with application leads to promotion. You have to be willing to say "God, before you promote me please make sure that I am ready. Please help me to put my life in order through the leading of your precious spirit." In order for you to move forward and upward your heart must be humble. Before you reach new heights, your heart must reach new lows. A heart that's not humble is a heart that isn't ready for new heights. God loves you and has probably delayed you because he knows how dangerous life is for a person who skips steps. Maturity is obtained one step at a time. God is a God of order and you have to be willing to let Him order your steps. Skipping steps leads nowhere and ultimately leads back to step one. Think back at how many people you have known that skipped steps and had to start over again. Where are you today in your life? Are you living based on God's original intent for you?

Questions:

Why is it important not to skip steps?

What is out of order in your life right now?

What is keeping you from being orderly?

What can you do right now to better align your life to Gods order?

2

Chapter 2: *Seasons*

Most people in the world experience four seasons: fall, winter, spring, and summer. Each season has a particular climate and purpose. Our spiritual life parallels this to a large degree. Let's break down the seasons and what happens in each.

- Winter: Prepping
- Spring: Producing
- Summer: Producing and Profiting
- Fall: Pruning

Fall: Pruning

Most of us love the fall. It is a season that we begin to witness change – the weather becomes cooler, and leaves begin to grow on trees. These leaves change from green to orange, orange to yellow, yellow to brown, and brown to the ground. However, did you know that the trees that have these beautiful leaves are experiencing death while these changes are occurring? Here is the spiritual parallel: when God pursues us he starts with the death process of our sin nature and idols. He begins to put to death everything inside of you that is not like Him. This confuses many people. They have been taught that prosperity should come with conversion based on what they see on TV. Little do they realize that the only time prosperity comes before pruning is in the dictionary. God wants every branch, every fruit, and every leaf that is not like Him to fall. Did you notice that when you sincerely began to desire to follow him that your green and plush life began to change? You went from having a plethora of friends to barely one. You may have lost a relationship or a job. God goes after our idols and what is occupying the throne of our hearts. What is "falling" in your life right now? Chances are it's your idols, which is why pruning is essential. By default, we are sinners and have a lot of garbage on the inside. God wants to get this out by pruning. If your refrigerator had rotten food inside of it, would you just let it sit there? No, you would throw it away and clean it out. This is akin to God's pruning process. How does your life smell to God? Is your life a fragrance or an odor? What rotten food have you had lying around for years? Has lust been a huge issue in your life? How about pride and insecurity?

You are three parts: spirit, soul, and body. Your spirit gives you God-consciousness, your soul gives you self-consciousness, and your body gives you world-consciousness. In order for you to walk in step with God, pruning must take place in each department. It is difficult to bear ripe fruit if you are following false doctrines or if you love your pastor more than you love God; if you listen to bad music or watching perverted shows. It's hard for God to use a body that is sick and overweight. Satan has developed a system that aims to keep people from tapping into their full potential and into a thriving relationship with God. He knows that if he can get people in cycles of defilement then they will be too carnal to be used. Pruning takes cooperation and my cooperation determines the length of my pruning or healing. What does this look like? In order for God to effectively prune us, we must be still. We must accept what is going on in this current season and trust God with it. We can't squirm and be too eager to get through it. There is a reason why we are given anesthesia prior to surgery – unless we are perfectly still the surgeon cannot do his job. It's in the stillness that healing happens. If we keep wrestling with God while he is healing us it just prolongs the process. Another useful analogy is that of an athlete coming back too soon from an injury: if he doesn't rest and let it fully heal, he will be hurt for a longer period of time. Trust God when He isolates you and begins to remove things out of your life.

One of the biggest reasons that we wrestle with God is because of our idolatry. We want to hold on to everyone and everything that makes us feel special. Only God can fill the hole in your heart. Let's look at John 15 to help us better understand this principle of pruning:

15 "I am the true vine, and my Father is the gardener. [2] He cuts off every branch in me that bears no fruit, while every branch that does bear fruit he prunes so that it will be even more fruitful. [3] You are already clean because of the word I have spoken to you. [4] Remain in me, as I also remain in you. No branch can bear fruit by itself; it must remain in the vine. Neither can you bear fruit unless you remain in me. [5] "I am the vine; you are the branches. If you remain in me and I in you, you will bear much fruit; apart from me you can do nothing. [6] If you do not remain in me, you are like a branch that is thrown away and withers; such branches are picked up, thrown into the fire and burned. [7] If you remain in me and my words remain in you, ask whatever you wish, and it will be done for you. [8] This is to my Father's glory, that you bear much fruit, showing yourselves to be my disciples.

In this passage are a few words that stand out: Gardner, branch, prune, and fruit. Each of these are pivotal to understand. Let's begin with Gardner. Jesus says I am the true vine and my father is the Gardner. The statement, "I am the true vine" implies that there are other kinds of vines. A vine is a stem inside of a branch by which nutrients for the fruit on the branch run through. It is similar to our veins - they have blood running through them which contains nutrients that are beneficial to our organs. A vine is just as important as our veins because if there is a clog in the vein our body won't receive the necessary nutrients. In life there are multiple types of vines. Money can be a vine, relationships can be a vine, approval and recognition can be a vine - anything can be a vine. Your vine will determine the size and the ripeness of your fruit. Jesus lets us know in this passage that He is the true vine and the ultimate source of everything good. There may be other sources that provide for your needs temporarily, but he provides your earthly and eternal needs.

Many people are striving in their singleness or in their married life for temporal and earthly satisfaction. They are looking for more opportunities, more money, and more love but what they fail to realize is that their external life is only as good as their internal life. The health of your fruit is only as good as the health of the vine that provides it. If your vine is false then your fruit will be as well. Take a look at the fruit from your life - how does it look? Are you happy? There are a lot of people that seem to have it all appear happy but they are empty on the inside. They may have everything but they don't have a relationship with God. I would rather lose everything and have God than have all of the outward trappings of success and not know Him. Life is not about surplus it's about access. If you have access you have surplus. If you have access to God you have access to everything...period! He is the true vine and the ultimate source - nothing on this planet can heal your broken heart. The best person to fix anything is the manufacturer because the manufacturer made the product and knows everything about it. God is the manufacturer and He came down to earth in human form and became our sacrifice.

He is the Gardner and what a great Gardner He is. A Gardner is a caretaker and a protector, a person who has the future in mind, a person who does what it takes to ensure that fruit is produced. God knew that Adam and Eve were going to fall and He also knew that Satan was going to do what he was going to do. He knew it all beforehand but let it happen because if the world was perfect, there would be no need for a perfect God. In order for perfect love to be shown there has to be imperfection; in order for perfect healing to be shown there has to be imperfection; in order for perfect salvation to be shown there has to be imperfection; and in order for provision to be shown there has to be imperfection. Love can only be proven when there is an opportunity to deny it which is why God placed the tree in the garden. Love is only proven when there is an opportunity to deny it. Right now there is a tree in the midst of your life that is tempting you to eat from it.

Verse two says that, "He cuts off every branch in him that bears no fruit while every branch does bear fruit he prunes so that it can bear even more fruit." God cuts off every branch in Jesus that is bearing no fruit. Bearing no fruit is a sign that you are not of Him. If you aren't bearing love, patience, kindness or any of the fruits of the spirit or don't have a heart that desires to, then chances are you are not of him. Salvation is a process and no one will be perfect in any of these categories but you have to at least be progressing towards it. God doesn't care about perfection – He cares about progression. Are you progressing? The Bible continues to read that every branch that bears fruit He prunes so that it will be even more fruitful. He prunes you so that you can be more loving, kind, and patient. You have to understand your life isn't yours and even if it was yours you wouldn't know what to do with it. We have tried for years to make our lives better but we always fail because nothing on the outside can heal a broken soul except the blood of Jesus. You can get married to the most handsome man or the most beautiful woman, but there will still be something lacking in your heart. No man or woman can heal your soul.

Your life belongs or is ruled by either Satan or Jesus. Are you of the kingdom of God or are you of the kingdom of the devil? The proof is in your fruit. Satan wants to use your God-given talents to produce fruit and results for his kingdom. He wants to use your voice, hands, feet, and mind to produce for his twisted kingdom. Satan and his cohorts love an unfinished soul that's not being pruned. They know that they will always feel empty and will always go to him to be filled. He wants unfinished souls to finish his work; unfinished singers to finish perverted songs; and unfinished people to marry. He wants broken homes and he doesn't want you to be pruned by your heavenly father. He knows that if you are left unfinished in your singleness you will have a greater chance of producing a bad marriage. He knows the issues that are produced from a heart left undone. Don't remain idle or try to run away from God's pruning hands. I know it can get lonely as a single person and even as a married person, but know that He is doing it for a reason - He is pruning you so that you can bear even more fruit. Cooperate in singleness and be pruned so that you can bear more fruit in marriage.

Jesus continues, saying, "[4] Remain in me, as I also remain in you. No branch can bear fruit by itself; it must remain in the vine. Neither can you bear fruit unless you remain in me.[5] I am the vine; you are the branches. If you remain in me and I in you, you will bear much fruit; apart from me you can do nothing. [6] If you do not remain in me, you are like a branch that is thrown away and withers; such branches are picked up, thrown into the fire and burned." We cannot do anything without him - we must first fall before we flourish. Remain in him.

Winter: Prepping

Winter is the season in a person's life when things are completely dead. No leaves, no fruit, no life. It can be cold, lonely, and bitter. However, this season in your life as a single person is pivotal. Things have to die in order for something else to live. An example of a winter season would be when you want to be married but are single, have no job, your friends have moved on and gotten married and are now having kids. Take heart though – winter can be a beautiful thing - it's a transitional experience. When something dies it moves onward. Many people look at the winter season as the worst but it is during this season that you are being prepared. When the ground is cold it is getting rid of all the impurities in the soil. This is so that when it comes time to plant, the soil is ready. Before a Gardner plants, he or she toils the ground which causes the ground to be bare as it heals. The ground purifies during this stage so that when spring comes and it's time to plant and produce, there will be nothing to hinder the process.

God toils before he plants and destroys before he develops. He has to in order for the right kind of fruit to come forth. Have you ever seen a field or a garden without a Gardner? It looks abandoned and unkempt. Everything in life must have something or someone tending it. If there is no one tending, then tragedy is imminent. You probably know of someone who is not being tended or a relationship that's not being tended; you can almost predict the outcome. Similar to a field full of weeds without a person tending it, so are our lives without God tending them. In order to walk with Him you have to deny yourself, let go, and allow death to happen. You have to die in order to live; so many people try and run from the pruning hands of God but don't run from him - run to him. Let Him prune you and let the coldness of winter purify you.

Spring and summer

Once the leaves have fallen and the cold winter has passed, the warmth ushers in spring and summer. Everything that happened in the fall and winter months sets the stage for what happens in these two seasons. Before growth, color, and fruit, comes death, isolation, and pruning. Nothing blossoms without pain or grows without turmoil and your life is the same way. People complain to God about this because they believe that life is supposed to be easy and without pain. However, pain is necessary for growth. During these two seasons of life, you begin to see fruit developing. Before your life blossoms it must die. It takes a lot to prepare newness and it takes a lot to strengthen the branch to hold the fruit. People want fruit but their branches are not strong enough to hold the fruit that they want to bear. If you want to bear big ripe fruit you must go through death, isolation, and pruning. You can't have the end without a process and the process was designed to ensure fruit grows. No process, no fruit. So many people want to have big fruit but they have weak branches. When a branch is too weak to handle the fruit the branch will break. Right now you may be thinking that you are tired of suffering and waiting, you want the fruit now. I know the feeling but these light afflictions are only for a moment and will not compare to the joy that's set before you.

I did a periscope today June 6th 2016 where I talked about going from milk to meat. The video is still up and if you have time go and check it out. In that video I talked about maturity and how God demands and desires growth from His people. I discussed why so many people want a lot but are not willing to work for it, or they have false expectations about what they can handle. No one starts lifting 200 pounds right away - you have to build up to it a few pounds at a time. No father or mother will hand their 5-year-old the keys to their new car, so why do we expect God to give us something that we are not mature enough to handle. There must be a process. You have to embrace each season and let God develop you so that when the season changes you will have strong branches to bear the fruit. Everyone wants spring and summer but you can't have either without fall or winter.

The season of singleness is a gift and God wants to make sure that you are prepared. There is a certain weight that comes with marriage and success – you can't just jump in without the proper preparation. A lot of people want to be married and successful but fail to realize the responsibilities that come with each of those.

Marriage was designed for mature people who take marriage seriously. Marriage is nothing to play with. We've all heard horror stories about marrying the wrong person or not being prepared. I am no expert, but I have learned to observe and learn, even if I am not in that particular season. One reason why most people fail at marriage is due to poor preparation and the negligence of their single life. If you aren't prepared, the infatuation stage will be too heavy for you. People say that they fell in love but no one does such a thing. People fall into infatuation not love. You grow into love. God designed love to have a process similar to the seasons I spoke about earlier.

The process begins with dying to yourself and becoming more selfless. It requires isolation meaning it requires you to learn how to love by spending time with God.

Everything in life has a purpose and the mismanagement of a thing or a person's purpose leads to abuse. Everything in life has a purpose and everything in life has meaning. When a person or thing loses meaning in the eyes of the beholder, that person or thing is now in position to be abused and misused. Many of us have defined things in life wrongly and have adopted ideologies and lifestyles that are keeping us from maximizing where we are. There is a purpose for your singleness and there is a purpose for God hiding you from the pursuit of any man or from any prospects to pursue because he wants you for Himself. He wants to prune, prep, and position you but how can he if you don't understand the purpose of singleness? Before we dive into this topic let's look at the definition of purpose. Purpose is why someone or something was made.

Singleness, like marriage, has a purpose and to find that purpose you have to consult the One who created it. God knows the original intent of everything that He made. Not only does He know the original intent of what He made, but He has our best interests in mind. A lot of people in our world today are unaware of the benefits of being whole. Unfortunately, a lot of people are full of holes and when a person is full of holes they are incapable of holding anything or pouring anything. They are always empty. No matter what is poured into them it flows out quickly. God desires for you and me to be whole and intact. Would you pour clean water or fresh juice into a cup with holes? Wouldn't you think it was strange if a person used a container with holes to water their plants? Then why do we think God is going to flood blessings into the life of a leaking soul? You have to ask yourself if you are willing to let God do surgery on your life? Am I willing to let God guide my heart so that when His blessings do come, they aren't wasted?

There is a problem in our word when it comes to the season of single life -we have mismanaged it. We have overlooked its God-given purpose. Due to mismanagement and negligence people are not prepared for the next level. How you engage with this level will determine if you are prepared for the next level. This is why the divorce rate is so high. People are not preparing for the next level and we aren't taking advantage of our single life. This problem masquerades itself throughout culture causing the deterioration of the gift of marriage. When people begin to reach out for what they are not prepared for they are setting themselves up to suffer consequences. Before you pray for anything, you have to ask yourself if you are ready and equipped for whatever you are asking God for. Pouting doesn't move God; preparation does. God could care less about any self-centered requests - He cares about resilience, fortitude, and Him being top priority in your life. God doesn't take idolatry lightly. Before He promotes you, He destroys your idols and any false perspectives you may have on marriage, love, sex, money, and. companionship, This is because He wants you to see your season clearly. In order for us to advance into maturity, we have to appreciate the level we are on. Many people complain about the level they are on instead of appreciating its benefits or the opportunity for growth. Right now you have the opportunity to increase your stock and to develop as a single person.

Instead of complaining about where you are, appreciate where you are. Let God show you what He wants to work in and through you. Your relationships are predicated on how well you and God are. If you and God are not on the same page, then neither will any of your other relationships. If God is not the core of your single life then how do you expect Him to be in your married life? God never forces himself on anyone - he is a gentleman and has nothing to lose. It is your responsibility to embrace your ultimate "best friend" and let him prepare you for the relationships and opportunities ahead. Take advantage of this moment because I'm sure any married person would tell you they wish they had more time as a single person. You have to remember that when you get married or into a serious relationship, your extra time is cut in half. When you have kids the time you have left is cut in half. The devil loves rushed relationships and rushed marriages because he wants your time. He wants your creative time cut in half and so consumed with the idea of love and not with who Love is. He wants you to rush into infatuation with the wrong person and allow the ambiance of it make you "feel" that this is from God, when it really isn't. Adam didn't receive Eve until he finished his assignment. Thus Eve was not presented to a restless Adam, but a resting one. Men, God will not bring your wife or lead you to marry a woman until you have finished naming your animals. Imagine if God brought eve to Adam with only 75% of the animals named? Most of the animals at that time would have been nameless. Adam's assignment would have been incomplete.

God doesn't care about "almost", He cares about completion. He knows that if He brings a potential Idol to a person who is not ready, then that idol will cause harm to that individual. God has given men an assignment that they must complete prior to pursuing marriage. Before God lets you pursue a woman He wants you first to pursue an assignment. It's in the pursuit of God and His assignment that teaches you how to provide and to protect. Before you can provide for and protect a woman you have to know who your ultimate provider and redeemer is. God wants you to know He is your provider and protector because He doesn't want you to go into a relationship the way the world does. The Bible says God saw that Adam was alone and then he made him a helper. God didn't forget to make him a wife, He was simply waiting for Adam to finish his assignment, which was naming the animals. He wants us to finish naming our animals too so that we can be at rest.

Ladies, God put Adam to sleep. Never allow yourself to be pursued by a restless man but a man that rests in God. When you jump into a relationship with a man who is still trying to figure out what resting in Jesus is, you will be all over the place with him emotionally. A restless man is not a man equipped to lead - I know this firsthand. I was a restless man still trying to figure out my place in this world while pursuing women. This left all parties, especially the women, confused. I wasn't comfortable being alone. I was too eager for love I wanted love and all that came with it. Ladies, if a man isn't resting and ready then don't present yourself. Let God present you to your resting man. Men, don't initiate any pursuit when you know for a fact you are not ready to provide and protect a woman's spirit, soul, and body. You are the leader and you have to learn how to lead spiritually, emotionally and physically. You have to know the Bible and be emotionally stable. You will want to be physically fit too – all of this contributes to you being a good leader. When the fall occurred and Adam and Eve ate from the Tree of Knowledge of Good and Evil, God asked Adam, "where are you"? You have to let your season of singleness prepare you to be a leader. This will ensure that your wife or your soon to be wife will find confidence not in you, but with your walk with God. Imagine if Adam didn't blame his wife but took full responsibility. Maybe the world wouldn't be where it is today.

***

Idoaltry: *Where All Sin Finds Its Roots*

Idolatry is where all sin finds its roots. Everyone struggles with idolatry and most of us are unaware that it slowly kills us. At one time or another we have all loved someone or something more than God. When we do this, that thing or person becomes an idol. We believe that this idol will sustain us emotionally throughout our lives. There is only One who can sustain us and that One is God. As I always say, whatever source you are plugged into becomes your sustenance. If that source fails, then you fail. There are many potential sources we get plugged into that are temporal and we put before God, such as money, success, and people. The only source that can sustain us within time and eternity is God. When we make "resources" our sources we will constantly come away feeling empty. The formula is simple: God is the ultimate source and all other things are just resources. Life will become difficult when a person makes a resource a source. This results in a person trying to fill a void with something that was never intended to fill that void. Only God can. This happens all of the time – we put too much pressure on people and things hoping that they will do what only God can do. No idol that we make can hold the weight of the desires that flow from a depraved heart. We must ask ourselves who or what do we love more than God? If we love someone or something one ounce more than God then we are in the danger zone. All of us are guilty of this at one point or another in our lives. What is the one idol that you love more than God? What do you put before Him? This is easy to find out. Who do you spend the most time with? Do you watch TV more than you read the Bible? Where do you go first when you experience pain? Do you consult someone else or God? There is nothing on this planet that can sustain us like God can.

The Pain of Idolatry

There is no greater pain than when we are stripped away from our idols. Idolatry is subtle until it is provoked. Once our idols are attacked, we become aggressive, protective, and dismissive. That's why we avoid people who notice and warn us about our idols. We simply do not want to let them go. Until God is everything, you will idolize anything. Right now, today, let your idols go. We all become aggressive when idols are attacked but we have to be willing to let them go.

It takes faith to get rid of our idols because we are selfish. Idolatry breeds selfishness. Selfishness kills. There is a huge difference between selflessness and selfishness. By definition selfishness means that you are consumed with who you are and what you want and will use anyone to obtain it. Selfishness means I am self-centered and everything revolves around me. Selflessness is the opposite of selfishness Selflessness doesn't mean that I never think about myself – it's just that I think lesser of my carnal self. It means that not everything in life is about me, that I have more things to give than to receive, and that my heart should be more about giving than receiving. There is nothing wrong with self-care, but when you are consumed with yourself, you are selfish. Selfishness is at the core of idolatry; before we can move forward we have to lay our idols at the feet of God and deny ourselves.

Questions: Utilize your journal if need be.

Why does God hate Idolatry?

Why is being pruned so important?

Right now, do you love anything more than God... if so why?

Why can't the things you listed above sustain you?

Why is God's timing so important?

3

Chapter 3: *Bad Habits and the Baggage they Carry*

Bad habits by definition are negative behavior patterns that have been repetitiously practiced over time. Repetition is the mother of learning. We are the results of what we have repeatedly done. Right now, you are the result of what you have repeated over days, weeks, months, and years. It is very important for us to understand the power of choice and the power of influence. Whatever is currently influencing us will dictate the image that we bare. I have a formula for bad habits: bad examples + bad environments + bad explanations = bad expression. Let's first look at bad examples.

Bad examples contain two main ingredients: people and perspectives that aren't aligned with God's original design. The first ingredient is people. People can be bad examples of role models for manhood, womanhood, marriage, and friendship. When these roles are expressed poorly they influence young minds – these young minds eventually begin to mimic what they see. We cannot expect people to model something that they have never seen themselves. It is imperative that we become good role models and are careful in what we express to the world. The reason why we have bad habits and are poor role models is because we have mimicked bad examples ourselves. We also mimic bad perspectives. We have allowed ourselves to become indoctrinated by people who have yet to succeed at singleness, marriage, business, ministry, and the list goes on. Don't ask someone about a topic that he or she has yet to succeed in. For example, you wouldn't go to a Financial Advisor who does not have a proven track record of success with managing money. It's the same with us. We have to seek out people who have proven track records in godliness and integrity. When we surround ourselves with those folks, we will become like them.

All of us, whether we know it or not, are surrounded by role models. These can be good or bad. You will model the role of whomever you observe the most. Right now you are modeling the behaviors that were modeled for you in regards to manhood, womanhood, singleness, and marriage. In addition, keep in mind that other people are watching and modeling you. This is why it is imperative for us to seek out what God's word says about these things. What examples does God provide for us in the Bible that we can apply to our specific situation? The Bible talks about how the Holy Spirit points to Christ and we are supposed to be pointed to what he did and what he is doing. That is why Jesus said, "I only do what I see my Father do" because he was strategic in the way he went about things. He was able to calculate every step and not waste any time. He didn't entrust himself to everyone but only to a certain few. The best way to learn from his example is to make sure that you are in a loving, thriving, relationship with Him. Remember, whatever or whomever you consume the most will consume you. You will model that individual, for better or for worse.

What roles are you modeling and on a scale 1-10 (one being the lowest and 10 being the highest) how are you modeling those roles?	
1.	#
2.	#
3.	#
4.	#
Who are your top role models and on a scale of 1-10 how are they modeling those roles?	
1.	#
2.	#
3.	#
4.	#
What can you improve in the roles you are modeling?	

Bad Environments

Bad environments can result from our choices or circumstances beyond our control. There are certain environments that we have no control over, such as the family we were born into and the economic status of that family. However, there are also bad environments that are created by our own choices. Many people choose bad environments due to their baggage, internal struggles, or simply curiosity. These choices include choosing friends, where to live, and who to marry, etc. Many people are suffering from the consequences of choosing bad environments. Some have even lost their lives. Ask yourself if you are choosing the right environments? It is crucial to use sound judgment and the wisdom God provides through His word. So choose well. Now, let's look at the environments that we didn't choose.

God knows exactly where He has planted you – you are not an accident. He placed you in your family for a reason even though you may not fully understand why. Time has a way of revealing why we were planted where we were. I don't care how bad the conditions were – He knows just how to turn things around for your earthly and eternal good. Even though the memories may be painful and you still struggle with them, He can heal you. You have to accept that you live in a fallen world with fallen individuals. They will hurt, disappoint, and neglect you. However, there is one person who is always present and desires to mold you, using everything in your current environment to accomplish His purposes. Remember the words that Jesus spoke on the cross when he said, "Father, forgive them for they know not what they do." You have to ask God to help you forgive those who have hurt and disappointed you. You have to be thankful that you survived and that you wouldn't be who you are today had you not gone through what you did. I am who I am today because of my bad days, not my good ones. Bad experiences have a way of either making us better or bitter. However, even if our environment is bad, we have to make a conscious decision to choose to be better and not bitter. Today you have to forgive others, not to set them free but to set yourself free.

Right now, at this very second, you have a choice to either be a product of your environment or make your environment a product of you. For an example of this we can look to Jesus. He did not allow the environment of the world to shape him. He allowed his presence to impact the world. He came in this world and, through his presence, he impacted the world. Right now, if you are a believer, you have power through the Holy Spirit to change whatever environment you are in. Greater is He who is in you than he who is in the world. No matter where your foot treads or where it is placed, you can change the climate. That's why the devil wants us to be oblivious about our environment. He wants us to be consumed by it. Instead of tapping into the precious spirit that is inside of us, to change the environment around us, the devil wants us to be prideful of this world and our environment. The Sprit of God in us is the most powerful thing on this planet. It's sad that we ignore it.

List below the environments you are predominately in? (Work, church, school, home etc.)
•
•
•
•

In what ways are you impacted by the environments above both negatively or positively?	
Negatively:	Positively:

In what ways through Christ could you impact those environments?

Bad Explanations

When we seek and receive bad advice we end up with bad explanations. Not all advice is good advice, nor is it always from God. To be clear, not everyone around you wishes you harm - I am sure that your parents and friends are good people. However, just because they are good people does not mean they will give you godly advice. There is nothing wrong with consulting those close to you, but you must consult God first. Before you go to the phone, go to the throne. Seek God through prayer and through his word. If you are consulting someone for advice, ask God for discernment when listening. Ask Him to guide you into all truth. Bottom line, you have to ask God what He thinks first. God is your number one consulting firm.

Have you even taken the necessary amount of time to seek God before you ask someone for advice? We are much more likely to seek people that we can reach quickly – people that are easily accessible and we know. Even though Wal-Mart may not have the freshest produce, it is close by and comfortable to go to. It is more difficult to travel further out to get the freshest produce around. It's the same thing when it comes to us when we need advice. It's so easy to pick up the phone and call someone you know who will tell you what you want to hear. It is much more difficult to pore through Scripture, be still, pray, and wrestle with an invisible God for answers. Many of us have allowed our lives to be the expressions of bad explanations. Many people are not explaining things to us from a healed, godly place, but from a hurt and wounded heart. Make sure that you do not surround yourself with the counsel of hurting people. There are two things to remember when seeking the counsel of someone: make sure that individual is successful and that their wounds have been healed in the area you are seeking advice in. You have to be willing to be still and ask God before asking anyone else. It doesn't matter if they give you good explanations, it has to be from God. Even though God can speak through anything – people, places, and things – we have to be still enough inside so that we aren't easily moved. God wants us to be still, not impulsive. Right now people are expressing themselves due to bad explanations that they received on marriage, sex, manhood, and womanhood. People are afraid of these things due to those faulty explanations. Again, bad explanations come from people who are hurting and haven't yet healed. This is why I do not seek counsel from someone who is hurting. When you surround yourself with hurting people, their wounds hinder you. Their wounds will hinder singleness, personal development, and the way you think about marriage.

Again, bad examples, bad environments, and bad explanations lead to bad expressions. Today I want you to look at the environment that you chose and the environment that you didn't choose. Today I want you to look at the people you go to for council. Do they give you good advice or "God" advice? Before moving to the next chapter we have to understand internal baggage.

The reason that we have bad expressions and bad habits is because we are bruised. We all have baggage. What is baggage? Baggage results from these things: hurts, disappointments, pain, eagerness, fear, frustration, and excuses. These are the biggest impediments to our success. Many of us are still bruised by the pain of our past, the pain of a breakup, or the pain of someone who abandoned us. I know for a fact that God is still healing me from the hurts of abandonment. I have been abandoned by a lot of people. These are people who I have given my heart, wisdom, time and resources to and have up and left me at the times I needed them the most. I know firsthand what that type of baggage can do to someone. If I don't get rid of my abandonment issue now then it will spill into other areas of my life such as marriage. I will want to constantly know where my wife is going and if she is going to leave me. I will expect her to heal wounds that she can't. This will result in excessive neediness and be a huge strain on my marriage. Now we are going to look at another area that brings baggage: disappointments.

All of us have been disappointed and let down at different times in our lives. Satan loves to use these so that we will doubt God and lose belief. He knows that if we divulge all of our trust to human beings that can disappoint us over and over again, that we will eventually project that to our view of God. "If they hurt me and God made them, can I really trust God?" That is a lie from hell. God is incapable – *incapable* – of disappointing us. He is always faithful – the problem is us, not Him. We begin to have false expectations and make demands on God because we don't take time to get to know Him. We don't take the time to figure out His rhythm, or His timing. God is not obligated to give us anything and unless we understand that we have more because of Him, we will never feel the joy of Him being our strength.

Satan also wants us to be eager. Eagerness causes us to accumulate baggage because it leads us into situations prematurely. Situations that we cannot handle nor are we ready for them. Impulsivity is also related to eagerness; they are like brother and sister. When we are impulsive we are basically telling God that we could care less about being molded or developed – we want it now. Instead of waiting on Him and casting restraint, someone who is impulsive only cares about what he see and desires. Spending solid alone time with God is always an answer, but it especially is for those of us who are impulsive. It helps calm our thoughts and think critically before making a decision. God must heal this or it can cause us to run over and ruin our families by skipping important stages, which can lead into dangerous situations.

The next way we accumulate internal baggage is through fear and frustration. Many of us are paralyzed by fear – whether real or imagined. These fears make us eager and anxious and cause more problems. Fear has an acronym: "False Events Appearing Real." What in your life right now is causing you to drift from faith toward fear? Many people are afraid to embark on the journey to find God's purpose for their lives due to fear. Excessive fear causes internal baggage, which causes us to become *needy and pull down the people around us. Frustration is another emotion that can* cause internal baggage. Frustration causes us to be impulsive and anxious. The enemy loves for us to make decisions based on frustration and impulse instead of solid facts. Satan and his demons know how to make your mind boil over with toxic thoughts and emotions. He knows how to get you to brood over a situation for so long that you become irritated by it and want to explode. This irritation will keep you in a cycle of bad habits, which will lead to more frustration and irritate the people around you. Don't allow fear and frustration to immobilize you.

Now I want to talk about the biggest hindrance to overcoming all of the emotions that create baggage: excuses. Excuses are one of my pet peeves. I especially hate it after I have explained a liberating point of view. It's sad that so many people are far away from their purpose due to the excuses they make. Excuses lead to extinction. The more excuses you make, the closer to extinction your purpose becomes. In order to tap into your full potential, you have to turn your excuses into execution. What I mean by that is instead of making excuses, make a plan and execute on it. A dream without a plan remains only a dream.

All of the things listed above that cause bad expressions and bad habits - hurts, disappointments, pains, eagerness, frustration, fear and excuses – are the reasons that people in our society are drowning in rivers of pain. Are you still hanging on to the pain that resulted from a broken childhood? Did you grow up in a single parent household with no father or mother to go to your games? These things become hindrances and have disastrous consequences in relationships. That is why single people *and* married people need to remember that their spouse or significant other cannot heal them from these things. They cannot unpack these bags. In order for you to be prepared for marriage, you need to make sure that God has unpacked all of your bags. If you are married and haven't dealt with your baggage, God can still heal you and make your marriage shine. So today, look in the mirror and examine yourself. What are your hurts and fears? What needs to be dealt with prior to entering into a relationship and then a marriage? God wants you to address these.

Take some time to reflect on the questions below alone or with a group and take some time on the next page to really write from your heart to God about your bad habits or the baggage's you may be carrying.

Reflection Questions: Group or Alone

- How do you handle disappointments?
- What are you eager for?
- What is causing you to be afraid and or frustrated?
- What excuses are you making right now that is causing your dreams to be extinct?

Reflect and write from your heart to God about your issues and fears.

God is near to the brokenhearted – Psalms 34:18

4

Chapter 4: *Image Bearers*

Each and every one of us right now are bearing an image. We are either bearing the image of God or the image of this world. The image that you bear right now did not develop overnight – there was a process that took place over many years. There was a beginning. Here is the way image develops – whatever influences you determines your identity, and whatever determines your identity determines the image you bear. Let's take a look at potential influences on your identity. There are two types of influences: outer and inner. In your outer world, you are influenced by images from the media, people you are friends with, co-workers, etc. I can tell you what your dominant influences are right now. Look at your call history, your online search history, the shows you watch, etc., who you go to in a crisis. These are your top influences. We have to be extremely cautious about who our influences are because these will begin to shape our identity.

The second type of influences are those that develop our inner life. These are your own past, disappointments, fears, your ego and ambitions. These influences are like rushing rivers that collide with the walls of our heart, forming an image on the inside of us. We fail to realize that our hearts are like sponges – whatever we allow to come in through our five senses – see, hear, taste, smell and touch – will shape us internally. An identity is crafted based on what we take in and it could corrode everything that God intended us to be.

Satan is cunning – he knows that whatever we allow to operate within our personal space and dominate our time will shape us. Ask yourself what you are spending your time on and who you are spending your time with. I want you to look at the movies you watch, the shows you watch, the places you are invited, and your search history on the internet. Look at them with discernment and make sure that you are seeing them for what they are.

Ask yourself if you are pleased with the image that you are bearing. If you aren't satisfied with your image, then take the time to ask God to help you reshape it. He is faithful to do this – it is never too late to take a U-turn and go back in the right direction. This process will always be difficult because we have what is called a "sin nature." We are always inclined to follow this nature rather than do what is right. The first step is willingness and it is a big one. As soon as you are honest with yourself and willing to change, God is faithful to do it. Are you willing to cut off every false influence that is causing you to bear a false image? It is your choice and your responsibility to ask God for an identity makeover.

Questions:

What are your top outer influences?	What are your top inner influences?

How are these influences shaping your identity?

Are you pleased with the image you are bearing if not what changes do you need to make?

5

The Bible says in Isaiah 40:31, "But those who wait on the Lord shall renew their strength; they shall mount up with wings like eagles, they shall run and not be weary, they shall walk and not be faint." (NKJV) This scripture is essential for each and every one of us that are waiting. It doesn't matter what you are waiting for – it could be a relationship, an opportunity, a career, a ministry – this verse is pivotal. In this context the word "wait" does not mean sitting. It is talking about walking and serving. Many people are "sitting" on God when God wants you to wait and serve Him. What is the promise if you wait on the Lord? God will renew your strength. Our strength isn't renewed when we are just sitting. Our strength is renewed when we are serving God and asking God what it is that He wants us to do. When you have that mindset and motivation your strength is renewed. Many people are waiting on that special person instead of waiting on God and letting him develop them first. Remember what I said earlier about promotion .God develops and prunes before He promotes .We have to be so consumed with our purpose and whom God made us to be that we have no time to fret over what or who we don't have. God's presence is enough to fill the void. However, this again falls on our shoulders. It is our responsibility to tap into God's power and allow His spirit to fill us. Look at cell phones for example. If you do not pay your bill, your service will be disconnected. However, this *does not mean that there is an absence of service.* It just means that you no longer have access to it because you haven't paid your bill. This is similar to what happened 2000 years ago. Your debt was paid which now gives you access to God, but you have to be willing to accept the payment so you can now allow God to fill your empty space. When you are consumed with God's purpose for you there is no time to worry about what you don't have. Have you paid your spiritual cell phone bill today? Repentance is all you have to pay.

Waiting requires us going to God and asking Him what He wants for us today. Every day that we are above ground we have to ask God *first thing* for direction. This means that before we go to work, before we serve our spouse, we seek His guidance. We have to ask Him what He has for us today. His presence will then begin to flood your life and fill up all of the idle space in your mind. Remember, an idle mind is the devil's workshop and Satan's demons know this. God doesn't want you to sit anywhere but at His feet. The only time you should be sitting is when you are at His feet or you are producing something at work. I cannot emphasize this issue of an idle mind enough, so please listen. This type of mind can lead us to idle hands, which then leads to idolatrous, wicked places. For some men, this may lead them to a pornography addiction. Porn is stimulating to the mind. Remember, the onus is on you. Unless you choose to let God's presence fill your idle mind, it will not happen. Let's talk about exactly what needs to be done to allow God's presence to fill our minds.

Before you can be able to maximize your time, you have to have a regiment in place to ensure that God gets the first fruits of your time. When you wake up, what is the first thing you do? Do you reach for your phone or do you reach for your Bible? I always tell people to charge your phone in another room while your Bible rest next to you, so that when you wake up the first thing you can reach for is your Bible.

What are you doing today to make sure that you have no idle time and do not drift from God? The Devil knows that if you have idle time your mind will drift. If your mind drifts, then your life will slowly drift away as well. Are you occupying that idle time with serving God? Most of us are hurting because we are waiting, sitting, and doing nothing. I tell people all of the time to get productive. Make no mistake, there is a difference between being productive and being busy. Busy has an acronym: "Being under Satan's yoke." Busyness is filling your life with a bunch of what I call "stuff and fluff". We fill our lives by clinging to this person or watching our shows, or looking at Facebook all day. We have no specific plan that we are following to ensure that we are productive. Productivity has an end in mind. You are producing specific things with a purpose. You are contributing to society. Productivity only comes with disciplining yourself. You have to discipline yourself by allowing God to lead you into all truth and serving Him. When you occupy that idle time with God, you will want to spend your time developing yourself, your purpose, and your relationship with God. You won't have any time to worry because you will be productive and have a purpose. Distractions and busyness corrode our focus. When a person loses focus he or she sinks. Case in point: Peter. He began to walk on water that was destined to drown him, but he focused instead. The reason why you are drowning today is because you have lost focus on Jesus. When Peter kept his eyes on Jesus, he began to walk despite the fact that he could drown. However, once he took his focus off of Jesus, he was sunk. The moment you begin to look at the waves and storms of life instead of your Creator, you will sink. Be productive in serving God and you won't have idle time.

Let's dive deeper into Isaiah 40:31, specifically the phrase, "they shall mount up with wings like eagles, they shall run and not be weary, and they shall walk and not faint." All of these phrases are "action" phrases, not "sitting and doing nothing" phrases. How do you "mount up with wings like eagles"? You do this by serving God. When you serve God, your strength will be renewed, you will have height to you and you will run and not be weary. As soon as life stabilizes, you will be able to walk and not run. You will not faint because wherever God wants you to go you will have the strength to get there. You go nowhere when you're sitting or are stagnant. Due to being stagnant, many people are bypassed by God because He knows that they have no intention of going where He wants them to go. Rest assured that God has a place for you to go. In order for you to get there you have to have strength, you have to be able to raise up on wings like eagles; run and not grow weary, and even walk at times. The Devil wants you to sit and wait while life passes you by. He wants you to be so focused on that thing or person that you miss the things that God has for you to do. God is always moving, always active, always running, always walking, not stagnant. When you engage God and begin to serve

God, the holes in your life will be filled. You will be whole and not filled with holes. You have to be so engaged with God that you do what he wants you to do and go where he wants you to go that particular day. When an eagle mounts up, when a person walks and runs they are ready to go somewhere. However, you cannot go anywhere without having your strength renewed. Your strength is not renewed by sitting and waiting for God to move. You renew your strength by moving with him and serving with him.

Look at yourself in the mirror and ask what is keeping you from moving and serving. Today is the perfect day to take the opportunity God is giving you to renew your strength. You do not build strength to stay stagnant – you build strength to move. You cannot do what God wants you to do without strength. God wants to give you this strength but in order to do this you have to engage with him. This allows you to go where God wants you to go. God often tells me to not worry about where He sends me because He will give me the strength to go. As long as God is involved, you will have the strength you need. Another benefit of strength is endurance. Endurance is key because you will need endurance in order to endure marriage, personal development, and your ministry. Endurance will help take you to the next level whether it is relationship, marriage, or ministry. God has a purpose in building your strength today so don't sit around and let life pass you by. Ladies and gentlemen, do not wait for your spouse and do nothing. Don't wait for people to show up to hear what you have to say – go to them. But before you go to them, go to Him and let Him guide you the rest of the way. God wants to build you while you are waiting. Turn your waiting into waiting.

Questions:

Why is it important to be productive?

Why is it dangerous to be idle and/or busy?

Where in your life are you idle?

Take some time in this box to develop a "Waiting/ Productive Plan". Think about what you can do daily to better serve God while he works on the rest of your life.

6

Chapter 6 – *Why Am I Here?*

Every one of us has a purpose. In order for you to progress and be productive, you have to have a purpose. Many people are trying to progress without a purpose. Instead of embracing God's purpose for today, they are looking for the purpose of tomorrow. We have a purpose because we are fearfully and wonderfully made. We were created for a time such as this. Even though this may not seem like the right time, it is – the time is now. God placed you here at this very moment for a reason. It doesn't matter where you grew up, who your parents were, or what you have gone through. Even though you may be placed here, it doesn't mean that you were placed and forgotten; He knows exactly where you are. That is why it is paramount for you and I to know why we are here. Here and there are two pivotal words – you cannot spell "there" without "here". Many people are overlooking "here" because they are too focused on "there". God has you here for a reason. Where are you today? Where is your "here"? If you do not manage *here* well then you won't manager *there* well. Ask God to make you and mold you right where you are. God has to take you through certain stages to take you to the next level and unless you learn to live in the here and now, you will not make it there. Remember, God promotes once you have mastered your present level. Many people get distracted including myself. I felt like my ministry would never take off, that I wouldn't get married, etc. I am so worried about tomorrow at times that I forget the One who holds tomorrow. We will always struggle with trying to get *there* instead of being *here.* This can be managed however – we just have to be in rhythm with God and work cohesively with Him. If you lose sight of your purpose for today then you will never get to the purpose of tomorrow.

There are seven "P's" of purpose: *Person, Perception, Purpose, Passion, Preparation, Proximity, and Position*. In order for me to know and walk in my purpose, I must know the person of God. In order to know the purpose of our singleness, marriage, career, etc. we must know the person of God. He isn't a machine; He is a person – this means that He has functions like us. If He has functions like us, it means that He has a personality, emotions, and thoughts. We actually function more like Him than He does us. However, when we understand that He is a person and wants to have a relationship with us – this changes us. He is so vast that he has the ability to be the God of the universe as well as your God. Do you know Him? There is a huge difference between knowing about Him, and know Him personally. Most of us are just content to know about Him; we aren't eager to actually *know* Him.

We have to learn to seek His face and not just His hand – we need to see who He is as a person. When we know Him as a person and how he wants to present himself to us individually, we will begin to know our purpose even more. When you begin to forfeit how you see things versus how God sees things, your perception of God will change. You will want to please Him. You will understand Psalm 39: "delight yourself in the Lord and He will give you the desires of your heart." What you delight in most or spend the most time thinking about will dictate how you see. God doesn't just care about what you see, but how you see it. He cares about *how* you view or *perceive* manhood, womanhood, ministry, you career, marriage, etc. Perception is a neutral word – you can have a right or wrong perception of something. God wants you to see life accurately. In order for you to get to the place that God has for you, you will have to have the correct perception of life. Each and every one of us has things along the way that affect the way we see things. How much time you spend with God will determine how you see things. Many of us right now are on the wrong side of the road when it comes to how we see things. We have a flat tire and a broken transmission. The reason why is because we have picked up incorrect views along the way that affect our perception of life's issues. These views include marriage, manhood, womanhood, etc. When you see things wrongly you will develop incorrect perceptions of them. Once you develop these perceptions, you will then act based on them. Eventually the way you really perceive things will manifest in what you do. We cannot "out-act" what we truly believe. The most important perception that we have in life is God. If we do not perceive Him correctly, then everything else is out of sync. Once we gain a correct view of Him through Scripture and prayer, we will begin to perceive life correctly.

Our past experiences play the biggest role in how we perceive life. Right now a lot of men have allowed their pasts to dictate the way they view relationships with the opposite sex and the same thing goes for women. We have so many holes in our lives because of our pasts. God gave you eyes in the front of your head for a reason – to see forward. God has given you the ability through His spirit to see forward *correctly*. In other words, if you obey God and take the time to get to know Him, you will perceive correctly. You will not be able to see things accurately until you sit at His feet on a regular basis, gaining more knowledge and understanding of Him every day. When you know the person of God and He has changed your perception, you understand your purpose – not just your overall purpose but also your day-to-day, specific purpose. You will begin to see the purpose of your singleness, marriage, career, and pain. People think that purpose is just this big, vague, spiritual thing. No. Purpose is in the details as well. Growth happens in details and God wants you to see all those details. He knows that how you handle the small things will determine how you handle the bigger things in life as well. You may have a big vision but if you don't understand the details or the little things, you cannot execute on that vision. This is why God wants you to focus on *here* and not *there*. Pay attention to the details and the purpose of every little piece that makes up the larger puzzle. This only comes when you focus on the here and now. When you focus on the details and get to know the person of God then your perceptions of yourself and others will change. Opportunities will pop up that you wouldn't have otherwise seen, but since you are now focusing more on the details you are able to take advantage of them. Your purpose will be clearer and once that happens he begins to build a passion inside of you.

Passion is force. Before He builds your passion for a thing, he builds your *compassion*. When God changes your perception, you will notice that your heart drifts towards something that seems to beckon you. Your heart is stirred towards something that you wouldn't have been able to see prior to letting God change your perception. Compassion is something that's asking for your passion to come towards it. God has a specific thing for you to be drawn to. So many people are distracted by carnal passions instead of being drawn by compassion. There is a need out there that you were created to fill. I remember the day that God gripped me while I was in my dorm room at Oral Roberts University. The phrase, "If you don't do this, what will happen to them?" repeated itself over and over in my heart. He then began to build inside of me a passion that I was drawn to. You have to be led there. Not everything that calls your name is the right thing. Until you perceive God accurately you won't be led to what He has for you. God wants you to be precise and direct – in order to get to your purpose you must see the details. In order for you to find your purpose you need fuel and that fuel is passion. You know you are passionate about something when you wake up at 3am thinking about it. You can't move until it is done. Once you find that passion the dam will break and it will flow uncontrollably.

You are the sum of your preparation.

Success happens when opportunity meets preparation. The reason why so many people aren't living in their purpose is because they are unprepared. You have to remember that preparation leads to promotion.

God always delays for a reason. He is putting you in the spiritual gyms of life for a reason. He knows that you need to be pruned and prepared before you can handle promotion. You will be put in places where you are forced to grow so that you can reach that next level. This process is illustrated in The Karate Kid. Mr. Miyagi taught Daniel valuable lessons about becoming a black belt fighter. He took him from the ground up – he followed a strict process. Mr. Miyagi knew that Daniel couldn't become a champion overnight. He gave him menial tasks to start off with in order to build his muscle memory. For example, in order to learn how to defend a punch, Miyagi taught Daniel a method that is now etched into pop-culture lore: "wax on, wax off." Over and over Daniel had to practice a waxing motion that would end up being one of his key weapons in battle. God is trying to do the same thing with you: He is teaching you techniques that you will need to know for your next season. Another prime example is the story of David vs. Goliath. God prepared David years and years for his battle with Goliath. Do you know how He prepared him? He taught Him how to be a good shepherd. He taught him how to dwell in His presence. He taught him patience. He taught him the little things so that David would be prepared for the big thing. David was in the messianic line, an important link in the chain that brought forth The Good Shepherd.

The reason why you are not defeating giants is because you aren't allowing God to prepare you. If David went into his fight with Goliath not knowing how to trust God, the result would have been different. He would have been nervous, and panicked. Instead, he calmly slayed Goliath. Do you see the process? This is why I don't get upset when demons attack me and things go wrong. It means that it's preparation time. God is using these things to prepare me and build my endurance. Before you present yourself to anyone, you have to allow God to prepare you. Your level of preparation will determine your level of success. It is critical to be able to notice this in your life – it will completely change your perception of difficulties and trials. You will have a new level of hope. Remember, seasons change. Once you have successfully navigated your season of preparation, you can move on to the next level. You are moving closer to your purpose.

Finding your purpose is a process and it takes time. You have heard the phrase "timing is everything." There is no better example in the Bible than Moses. He didn't find his purpose until he was in his 80's. He grew up in Egypt, God removed Him from Egypt, and then sent him back to Egypt to deliver His people. Along the way, Moses made some mistakes. He forced himself into exile when his compassion for the Hebrew people led him to kill an Egyptian.

God will test you by putting you within the proximity of your purpose. Before He puts you in the epicenter of His purpose, He puts you close enough to do it at a high level but far enough away that you don't mess it up. Look at this almost like a buffer zone. He is preparing you privately. He is getting you acclimated to the sun before sending you to the beach where there is no shade whatsoever. As I said earlier in the book, the preseason comes before the season. God puts you in the proximity so that you can have a greater appreciation and respect for what your purpose will eventually be. Purpose is key. When you know your purpose, you will know what spouse to choose because you can now be specific. Purpose clarifies things.

The reason that I am writing this book is to help you understand that YOU have to search out your own purpose. However, you cannot find your purpose without knowing God. This will shift your purpose from earthly to eternal. You will no longer see the need to store up treasures on earth, but treasures in heaven (Matt 6: 19-21). When your purpose is earthly, you will be bankrupt eternally. When your purpose is eternal, you'll be blessed in the afterlife and fulfilled on earth.

God did not create you for retirement – He created you for fulfillment. Are you fulfilled today? If you don't take the time to understand your purpose specifically and of life in general, you will continue to leak.

7

Genesis 2 lays the blueprint for manhood. Let's look at verses 15-17: "The Lord took the man and put him in the garden to work and to keep it. The Lord God commanded him saying, 'you may surely eat of every tree in the garden, but the Tree of the Knowledge of Good and Evil you should not eat, for in the day that you eat of it you will surely die.'" This Scripture illustrates beneficial truth for men. The first point is that God will give you an environment to steward before giving you a family to steward. Before we can steward a family and all that comes with it, we must first know how to steward our lives and our God-given assignment.

God will always put us in a place that he wants us to steward. In verse 15, God gave Adam the garden to work and keep it. Men are built to work and keep and God wants to teach us how to be an effective husband, father, and servant to the community. All men have a garden that they are supposed to tend to. Before we can lead a family, God gives us a garden to tend to in order to learn the principles of stewardship. There is a lack of good stewardship among men today. We have been self-centered for so long that we have lost the essence of what it means to work and keep. Many of us are good at *working* at something but not *keeping* something. God puts us in places to learn how to do this. Many of us men know how to get a woman but not how to keep a woman because we are manipulative. We only work to get her attention to satisfy our own desires for selfish gain. This is why God gives you an assignment first. The assignment that He gave Adam was to name the animals. Before he was able to name and exercise his purpose he first had to be placed somewhere to practice it. Before God places you in your purpose, you have to be placed into a garden to tend. Remember, stewardship is not working to grasp something but working to keep something. Don't squander the opportunities that God has given you to steward.

After God places us He gives us a command. We have to learn to hear from God because He will always give us instructions first. Men, the reason why we are leaking is because we don't know how to get patched. In order for us to lead and steward a woman we must be whole. The only way to get whole is to be filled with God. You can't drive a car with tires that leak air and you cannot lead a family if you are leaking spiritually.

Look what happened to Adam – he began to make excuses after the fall. God never told Eve what to do, he told Adam. He gave Adam the assignment. He primarily speaks to Godly men in relationships because we are the head of the home. When He speaks to us, we have to listen. We have to master the art of active listening.

Many of us men have heard God speak to us over and over again but have neglected to listen. Obedience is not just hearing but having the corresponding actions to follow. When God speaks to us we have to listen. In order for us to believe something we have to know that thing is valid. If we don't listen to God's voice then it means we don't believe its validity. If your heart is vain and sinful then you will not be able to perceive what God has to say.

God said, "make sure to eat of every tree of the garden but of the tree of the knowledge of good and evil you should not eat. For in the day you eat of it, you will surely die." God gives us liberty but his liberty has boundaries. We as men need restrictions and God's restrictions are designed to protect us, not steal our fun. Each and every one of us has a sin nature that is perpetually inclined to do the wrong thing. We have a skewed perception of manhood. God's boundaries don't mean that he doesn't want us to be great or ambitious. Many men are so ambitious that they allow themselves to stray beyond God's boundaries. God has boundaries for every level of your life. Don't allow your zeal to go beyond God's wisdom. God said that Adam and Eve could eat from any tree in the garden except for the tree of knowledge of good and evil. We have to make sure that we respect the restrictions within our garden. Sometimes God keeps a tree in the midst of our lives to keep us focused. Many of us want to eat from a tree that we have been restricted from due to our zeal.

As I mentioned earlier, God will always place a tree in the midst of our lives to test our commitment to Him. Just because you have a beautiful wife does not mean God is going to remove all of the beautiful women from your view. The main tree inside all of us is our sin nature. We have to make sure that we do not give in to its carnal desires. Don't allow your sin nature to lead you because, just like the tree, if you eat of it, everything connected to you will die as well. Before you are able to lead a woman or a family, you first have to be led by God.

Let's look at verse 18: "it is not good that man should be alone." Many of us think that we know when the right time is for us to not be alone anymore. Instead of waiting on God, we rush into and out of relationships looking for "the one." Instead of embracing God's presence in the midst of our loneliness we fight it. If we practiced staying in God's presence then we wouldn't have to worry about feeling lonely. When God is with you, He occupies the lonely space.

God has you alone right now for a purpose. You have to remember that your point of view is limited; God's is not. Many men have sacrificed their assignments to pursue a woman. They are consumed by the desire to have a companion and to have their sexual needs filled. If they would become consumed with God they wouldn't have time to worry about who their mate will be. Even though Eve wasn't provided for Adam until later, it was the right time. Only God knows if you need to be alone for a longer period of time. God has assignments from which He wants you to learn from prior to finding a mate. God will always give you an assignment before He gives you an assistant. He wants you to sacrifice for this assignment so that you will learn to sacrifice for your family. Many men are too self-centered to sacrifice themselves for Christ and a family.

She will be fit for you and your purpose

Take a look at verse 18: she will be fit for you and your purpose. Men, you do not know what is best for you when it comes to a woman. You don't have to have sex with a woman to find out if she is a good fit for you. God knows you better than you know yourself and He knows the right woman for you. She will be the right fit for you and your purpose. Many men are pursuing women who have no connection to their purpose, no connection to them, and aren't the right fit. You cannot force what doesn't fit – it should fit naturally and flow. Many people are married to the wrong person, but if they are willing to let God redeem their marriage, He will fit them to each other.

Let's look at verse 19: 'Now out of the ground the Lord God had formed every beast of the field and every bird of the heavens and brought them to the man to see what he will call them, and whatever the man called every living creature, that was its name. The man gave names to all of the livestock and to the birds of the heavens and to every beast of the field.' Verse 19 continues, "now out of the ground the Lord God had formed every beast of the field and every bird of the heavens and brought them to the man to see what he will call them' – the most important word in that sentence is the word "formed." Before God forms a man's wife or his future, he will form things in that man's presence. God is doing this to show you what you have inside of you. We were created in God's image and God blessed us all with a certain amount of creativity. God is the only one who can create something out of nothing, but he passed down a certain amount of creativity to us. God begins to form things in our lives to see what we would creatively call it. During your single season God is placing things in front of you to see what you would call them. God is giving you dominion and authority and wants you to follow him submissively. This is why you have to be very careful what influences you and allow inside of you – they will manifest in how you name things. There is power in a man's words - whatever you call will come to you and become what you name it. Before God gives you one of His daughters and a future, He's going to show you how to name things accurately. How can you call a woman beautiful if you are looking at other women lustfully? How can you call a woman a helpmate if you've only used them for your selfish desires? We must have the right perspectives of the gifts that God wants to give us prior to receiving them. God will give you tests on these things constantly to see how you perceive them. Men, you have to guard your words because they matter. They will have a huge effect on your future wife and children. We were created to be the leaders of the home. The Bible doesn't say women are to wash men with the "Word", but men are to wash women with the word. Your words will shape your future. To sum up, God will give you an assignment before He gives you an assistant.

God will send assignments your way to fine-tune your perspective and your words. God wants to create a man who is poised, not easily moved, and has self-control. The most important fruit for a man in this era is self-control. Men are easily lured by their pride and sexual desires. Before you marry, you must be self-controlled. Before you can lead a woman, a family and even yourself, you have to be led by God. A man led by God will become a leader. Following God requires obedience – as Paul said, we must be imitators of Christ and follow closely. Adam was not obedient when he ate the fruit – he dropped the ball. We don't know why, but he did. God did not tell Eve the requirements but He told Adam.

The Bible says that we have to be very careful what we say as men. What we speak into the universe we will become. If we talk poorly, stressfully, or recklessly, we will have that kind of life. Your words have to be specific and strategic, they cannot be loose and lackadaisical. Your words have power – God gave Adam the power to name all of the animals. This is a principle – your words have weight and they will determine your destiny. Change your words and you will change your life and the lives of your family. Your words have the power to *wash*.

There is something out there trying to reach you because you have given it license to come through your words. The Bible continues to read, 'the man gave names to all of the livestock and to the birds of the heavens and to every beast of the field.' The key words in this verse are "all" and "every." There is a certain stage in your life right now that God is keeping you in until you name "all" your animals. Many men have yet to advance because they haven't finished their assignments. God operates with decency and order. In order to progress you have to name all and every animal. You have to be poised and focused and ask God if your assignment is over. God will advance you once your assignment is over. Before He sees fit for you to not be alone anymore He will want to know if you finished *His* assignment. Any assignment left undone will hinder how your assistant assists you. If you have an unfinished dream or a restless mindset and aren't poised, you will become a burden to your wife. I tell men all of the time not to pursue a woman until he is no longer restless. A restless man is not poised, patient, nor productive; he's undone.

You have to be strategic enough to ask God to give you poise and patience so that you can be productive. A woman needs a man who is poised, emotionally stable, and patient. Women are wired differently than men – they can be overly emotional at times and need men who will be patient with them. As I alluded to before, patience is not just waiting – it is the attitude that we have while we are waiting. As men, God made us logical and strong, able to process everything that is thrown our way. Men tend to be less emotional than women. We have to ask ourselves why God wants us in this scenario, what does He want us to learn? We need to be productive because women want to follow productive men, not "parked" men. A lot of men are parked in their past sins and present situation which will cause them to have unproductive futures. Whatever you give a woman she multiplies, therefore if you are unproductive how is she going to assist you? Look at the relationship you are in right now? Is your spouse or partner frustrated with you or is she walking in faith with you? When you are positioned, placed, and planted, that woman will multiply your dream by a thousand, she will make you known in the streets and will make you a king. How can a boy become a king if he's still a boy? Are you allowing God to develop you so that you are strong enough for a potential spouse to lean on?

Questions:

Men, why is stewardship important and ladies why is it important to wait for a man that can steward his season?

Men, why is it important to know Gods voice and to obey his instructions and ladies why is it important to be with a man that can hear and obey God's voice?

Men, why is it important to give a woman something to maximize and ladies how does it benefit you being with a man that's progressive and not parked?

Men why does God give us an assignment before an assistant?

Men why are our words so important?

Fellas, take some time in this box to think about your assignment. Write down below what you know you need to finish before you pursue a woman and take some time to develop a plan to finish your initial assignment.

Let's look at verses 20-25 – 'but for Adam there was not found a helper fit for him so the Lord God caused a deep sleep to fall upon the man, and while he slept took one of his ribs and closed up it's place with flesh. And the rib that the Lord God had taken from the man He made into a woman and brought to the man. Then the man said, 'this at last is bone of my bones and flesh of my flesh, she shall be called woman because she was taken out of the man. Therefore, a man shall leave his father and his mother and hold fast to his wife and they shall become one flesh. And the man and his wife were both naked and not ashamed.'

The Bible talks about how man was made for God and woman was made for the man. When a woman understands that she was made for the man, then she will help him develop, diversify his abilities, and broaden his posture.

Ladies, a man needs your help in the following four ways: help him dream, develop, help his disposition, and help his dominance.

Let's look at helping his dream. You were created to help him make sure that his dreams become reality. This is a team effort – you guys are working together. However, before you endorse his dream you must make sure he is pursuing Christ. If he is following his own agenda, then you are not meant to multiply it. You were created to multiply a dream that reflects the image of God. You have to make sure that he is in tune with the Holy Spirit. How do you know if a man is in tune with God? You know for a fact that he is in tune with God based on his commitments. If he is more committed to his agenda and his ideologies, then he is not walking with God. If he is more committed to the religiosity of Christianity than he is to God, that is proof that he will break the commitment that he made to you. You were created to help his God-given dreams become reality. When a man dreams ambitious, God-given dreams he needs a woman to give him encouragement to fulfill those dreams.

You were also created to help his development. There are stages in a man's life when he is going to need a woman's understanding. Men want a woman who can understand his failures, fears, and faults. We need someone who is going to be a rock for us. a safe harbor. If we cannot come to you with our fears and frustrations, we will pull back and close up. Many women are so caught up in having to be strong that they dilute a man's confidence. Many women have damaged their men this way. A man needs his woman to be gentle and understanding. Do not get it twisted – a man needs a woman who is willing to tell him he's wrong and can give him tough love. Development is not only for peace, but for push. Men need a woman who will push with peace but not pull with problems. A lot of women come to their men and pull them with problems that clutter their mind. Do not give your king something that the queen can handle. Give God your problems and let Him direct you on how to present those to your man. If you are a single woman reading this book, you have to understand that your words must be gentle, not forceful. You have to be cognizant of the words you speak – they can frustrate him and point him back toward his fears. You were created to help him develop. Push him, but make sure that it's peaceful.

He needs you to help him with his disposition along with his development. You were created to help his back go wide, his neck stretch far, and his feet to walk with weight. In other words, you were created to help him be confident. The first place a man should go after seeking direction from God is his woman. He needs to be able to look in her eyes and know for a fact that she has his back. Are you talking behind his back or do you have his back? Are you focused on pushing him forward?

Lastly, you were created to help his dominance. You have to help him dominate his workplace and anything that he endeavors to do. God created the man and the family unit to be dominant. You were not created to constantly go through warfare and suffer losses and failures. God created us to have dominion.

When a woman becomes frustrated, oftentimes she will drift into something that gives her the ability to be strong in her own right. When Eve went by the tree, the serpent, asked her if God *really said* to not eat from the tree. Adam told this to Eve but he did a bad job of stewarding her with this information. Satan lured Eve into believing that she needed to be equal to God and thus eat from the tree. She drifted away from Adam. The best way to disrupt the steps of a man that's trying to push forward is to cause his woman to be frustrated. It is important for women to understand how Satan tailors warfare for them: he is always going to turn you against him and vice versa. If you want to be with a God-fearing man, you have to understand that you will be used against him because you are the one closest to him. When you are a man's vault and you have his heart, you can lure him. This is why the devil is after you – he wants your man to sacrifice his position of leadership. He wants the roles to be reversed – for you to be the leader of him instead of the other way around. Remember the garden? Eve took the fruit to Adam and instead of being a man and turning from temptation, he gave in and fell prey to Satan's game plan. Women will always be used to bring men down. Ladies, you have to ask yourself if you are a dangerous woman or a woman that will develop your man. Will you help him develop his dream, disposition, and dominance?

Let's look at verses 21-22: ' so the Lord God caused a deep sleep to fall upon the man and while he slept he took one of his ribs and closed up its place with flesh. And the rib that the Lord God had taken from the man he made into a woman and brought her to the man. '

Let's break this down. Women, make sure that you are peaceful; men do not like a woman who disrupts his rest. Don't think it strange when God begins to use things in your singleness to form you. While God is forming you, he's putting your man at rest. It's pivotal for you to become formed and developed. God is preparing you for the right man. As the preparation takes place inside and outside, you will become peaceful. The reason that God cannot make you peaceful is because you are restless in the season that he wants to do it. You have to understand seasons and the season is right now for

God to prepare you for marriage. He wants you to become peaceful so that you can bring that peace into a marriage. This is vital because men and women process things differently. Men process things internally while women process things externally. Ladies, it's easy for you to vent – you process while you are talking but a man processes quietly.

It's important for ladies to understand where the man was formed and where the woman was formed. God formed the man out of the ground, and God formed the woman out of the man. There will always be frustration between men and women. Women will wonder why men aren't as into them as they are into him. It's not that your man doesn't love you, it's that he was built to work, to build, to "go get it." I'm not saying that women cannot create their own ideas, businesses, ministries, etc. but what I am saying is that God has a plan of bridging two dreams into one dream.

Fellas, you have to make sure that you are balanced. You have to be strategic enough to allocate your time to the right places – your wife, son, daughter, family and your craft. You will often have to make sacrifices but know that God will teach you how do so. Ladies, you have to allow that man time to live, time to be in the ground, time to be outdoors. When you allow that man to form himself in what he was formed out of, it will bring him back peaceful. Many women want to keep their men close to them, to stay around the house or to go here and there with them but that pressure will only frustrate him.

Questions:

Ladies, why is it important for you to know where the man was formed from?
What can you be doing now to be prepared to enhance a man's dream, a man's development and his dominance

Why is it important to be a peaceful woman before being placed in a relationship and in what ways can you improve in this area?

Why is it important to be brought to a resting man?

Good communication and having proper expectations is key when it comes to dealing with people. Communication has become a lost art and most lack good people skills. People skills are essential, because how we interact with people will determine how prosperous we are. If we do not view people the right way then we will have poor interactions with them. We need people to help get us where we need to go. Communication is key. One thing that goes a long way in determining how we communicate is our expectations. Our expectations will determine our perceptions. By definition, perception is how we see what we see. Many people have the wrong perceptions, therefore they communicate poorly. Since we do not perceive people correctly, we begin to put false expectations on them. How do you see what you see? Do you see accurately? Do you see people through the lens of God's Word? If you perceive people in life contrary to the way God designed them to be seen, then your expectations of people will be inaccurate. Many people have lost relationships with good people because they had wrong perceptions of them. Men and women, no matter what age, have to perceive each other correctly to have healthy relationships. If their perception is off, false expectations and poor communication will abound.

Another problem with our world today is that people put God-like expectations on others and people-like expectations on God. He cares about how you perceive and know others – do you think clearly or are you confused? God is not the author of confusion – it's Satan, and he wants to confuse us through false expectations. If we put God-like expectations on others, we will break them. There is no other person on this planet strong enough to sustain you other than God. He is the source through which all resources flow. Men, you are not the source for women and vice versa. We are all resources and not sources. When a person puts a source-like weight on a resource, that resource will begin to break. The reverse of putting God-like expectations on people is when we put people-like expectations on God. We get aggravated at God and don't trust Him because we perceive him like man. We are disappointed at life's circumstances; we don't think that he will come through for us or even may abandon us. Maybe he won't use us in the ways we want to be used? Isaiah says that God's ways aren't our ways. That is why it is important to perceive correctly because if we don't, we will put false expectations on things due to us not understanding what those things truly are.

Perception and discernment are one and the same. God has given us his precious spirit that enables us to see beyond what our natural eyes can see. We cannot allow our perception to be defined by the World and how it wants us to see things. We have to constantly go to Scripture and ask God what He has to say about manhood and womanhood. What about marriage?   When I find out from Scripture how to see things, I will be able to communicate with others clearly.

In this section of the book we are going to talk about three key phrases: the process of developing poor communication skills, the effects of poor communication skills, and the power of good communication skills. Let's begin with the process of developing poor communication skills. This process is comprised of four "c's": culprit, compromise, content, and poor communication. The culprit is Satan and his world's system. His goal is for us to live contrary to God's original way and instead grasp on to his perverted way. He wants our lifestyle, mind, and our overall well-being to be perverted. He understands that if he can get us to adopt his ways of living then we will compromise God's ways. How many people in the world today have adopted Satan's and the world's way of thinking? When they adopt his way of thinking, they will compromise the standards of God. This will also cause deterioration on the inside of a person. How many people right now have things in their heart that they have yet to deal with? How many people still have bad content inside of them? When a refrigerator is unplugged from it's power source, the food inside of it will rot and cause a stench. How many people's hearts are unplugged from God, their power source? Is your life a fragrance or an odor to God and others? The state of your heart influences how you communicate. When the content of our hearts is corrupted, poor communication will result. The process of poor communication begins with a culprit, a person whose philosophies and ideologies are trying to infuse our way of living.

Matthew 15:10-20 talks about contaminated hearts and the poor communication that results. The Bible says, "and he called the people to him and he said to them, 'hear and understand, it is not what goes into the mouth that defiles a person but what comes out of the mouth, this defiles a person. The disciples came to him and said to him, 'do you not know that the Pharisees were offended when they heard this saying? ' He answered, 'every plant that my heavenly father has not planted will be rooted up. Let them alone, they are blind guides and if the blind lead the blind, both will fall into a pit.' But Peter said to him, 'explain the parable to us,' and he said, 'are you also still without understanding? Do you not see that whatever goes into the mouth passes into the stomach and is expelled? But what comes out of the mouth proceeds from the heart and defiles a person, for out of the heart come evil thoughts, murder, adultery, sexual immorality, death, false witness, slander. These are what defile a person, but to eat from unwashed hands does not defile a person."

The Pharisees in this text criticized Jesus and the disciples because they didn't wash their hands when it was time to eat. The Pharisees were a group of people who were so consumed with cleaning the external aspects of their lives, that they ignored the internal. They portrayed a life of perfection on their Facebook, Snap Chat, and Instagram accounts that they did not live on the inside. God could care less about what you look like on the outside; he cares about the content of your heart. When Jesus begins to talk to the Pharisees and other people, he said that so many people get consumed with exteriors like physical touch and hand-washing; however, it is what comes out of a person that defiles them.

What comes out of your mouth? Whatever those things are reflect what's in your heart. Out of the heart flow the issues of life (Proverbs). How many things have you cursed and damned because of your words? What aspects of yourself have you damned because you cursed yourself? You have to clean the inside of your heart to ensure that the words you speak are edifying. When you rebuke are you gracious? When you speak to a non-believer do you heap your beliefs on them? We have to understand the beauty of communicating gracefully. So many people allow the culprit and his lies to contaminate their hearts, which leads to poor communication. It's not what you engage in or what you touch that makes you defiled – it's what you allow to incubate inside of your heart. The process of developing poor communication is when we allow ourselves to adopt philosophies from the devil. When we allow ourselves to compromise the standards of God and our values, we allow bad content to develop inside of our heart. This leads to poor communication. People allow things to rot inside of their heart and this makes them spew over into rotten communication. A clean heart leads to clear and constructive communication.

The effects of poor or no communication

Where there is poor communication there is poor clarity. Where there is poor clarity, there is confusion. Where there is confusion, there are bad choices, and where there are bad choices, there is chaos. This world system is designed to cause us to communicate poorly. Satan and his demons understand the importance of silence. Silence becomes a dam to the river to which ideas flow. Communication is where help flows, ideas flow, insights flow. When there is a separation or gap or hindrance to that communication, people become confused and vulnerable. There is something damaging that happens when a person is not clear. When they aren't clear about expectations, they get nervous, then comes fear. Clarity is essential in every aspect of life. That's why I tell people to get clarity from God first because He has a perspective of your life and He knows everything about it. The Bible says in 1 Corinthians 14:33: "God is not a God of confusion, but of peace.' He is a God of clarity, insight, and wisdom. He won't lead you astray and he's going to make sure that there are no dams separating the flow. God is doing his part, but we have to do our part. If we have no connection with God, how can God flow through us so that we can communicate clearly? Many of us get into a phase of life where we just begin to assume without asking. Many people are engaging in relationships silently; they aren't communicating their fears, expectations, how they feel, or their faults and frustrations. When a person does not communicate those different things and their silence boils inside of them, then they will eventually blow their lid. How many people have caused chaos in other people's lives because they fail to communicate? Do not stay silent – always ask, don't assume. I would rather someone confront me and tell me what I need to know then assume and find out I know nothing. How many people are walking around with poor definitions and a poor understanding of people, assuming without asking?

Where there is poor communication, there is poor clarity. It is important for you and I to be clear. I tell ladies to make their expectations clear. Fellas, make sure you speak clearly. It is best to clarify things than to walk into a relationship blindly. You don't want to enter into a relationship with confusion. The bible says in James 3:16, ' for where there is envying and strife there is confusion and every evil work.' In the chambers of confusion there is evil. The two key words that we see in James 3:16 are "envying" and "evil work". When a person envies someone, the person that they envy does not know. When a person has strife against another, that strife is unknown. Once an interaction occurs between the two, there is confusion. Have you ever walked into a room and felt tension between you and another person and you didn't know what it was from? A lot of tension is conceived due to assumptions, envy, strife, lust, silent sins, hidden sins, and unspoken sins. What happens is that other people get confused based on your envy, strife, and manipulation. How many people through envying and strife have sabotaged somebody else's life? How many people through strife have committed murders, robbed, and done evil things because they assumed and kept silent? Confusion is where the enemy thrives and he knows that the best way to keep a church from advancing against his system is to keep them confused. Ladies and gentlemen, look at modern day Christianity. We argue more about doctrines than we do advancing God's kingdom. He knows that if he can keep the church confused and divided then he will have a better chance of winning. If you look at our world today, who is winning? We know that God is going to win in the end, but right now the church spends too much time quarreling about ancillary issues. There hasn't been much focus on unity. Confusion brings disunity. If I am confused, I couldn't finish this book. Confusion breeds bad choice.

Bad Choices

Do not act from confusion – act from clear communication and clarity. Before you act on anything, be confident that you know what you are getting into. Many of us make decisions from hurt. You might be in a situation right now where someone has hurt you. Make sure when you interact with that person, you do it from confidence and clarity, not confusion. When you make bad choices from confusion, you will find yourself in chaotic situations. What in your life is chaotic, unstable, unsettling, and bound by fear? Is it that you are communicating with others but not God? Is there something in your life that is keeping that communication from flowing?

Now let's talk about the power of good communication skills. There are four types of communication that determine good or proper communication: calm, constructive, committed, and concise.

There are two passages of Scripture that I want to talk about. The first is James 1:19-20 and the other one is Proverbs 15:1. James 1:19:20 says, "Know this my beloved brothers, that every person be quick to hear, slow to speak, slow to anger. For the anger of man does not produce the righteousness of God." Being quick to hear is pivotal when it comes to communication. We have to hear beyond what is being said. Most people do not hear to understand. When it comes to communication with someone you love, it is important that you are ready to hear before you are ready to speak. People are so consumed with trying to get their point across that they fail to acknowledge the other person's point of view. You have to first hear, then process, then speak. This passage of Scripture is encouraging us to be quick to hear beyond what is just being said – when we hear we have to use more than just our ears we have to use our eyes as well. You have to be able to look at someone's body language, get a feel for his or her mood, and put yourself in his or her shoes. Then let your compassion put you at ease. If you are in a conversation with someone you love, let love ease your point of view so that you can hear them. If you are hearing from someone that you love, their hurt is coming from the right place even if they misunderstand you.

Take the time to hear and be slow to speak

Being slow to speak is just as pivotal as being quick to hear. It's best to make sure that we speak after we have heard clearly so that we are responding from the right place. The next part of the verse is to be slow to anger. If I am quick to hear and slow to speak, it will cut my anger in half. Many people are going out of their way to speak from a place of bitterness and this is why it's pivotal that you don't just assume and that you don't allow bitterness or un-forgiveness to sit in your heart. Whatever you allow to sit in your heart will boil over into your conversations. Satan and his demons know that the best way to disconnect two people that love each other is for them to harbor emotions of bitterness and resentment towards each other. These emotions spark intense conversation – there won't be kind tones but tones of anger. We have to be slow to anger because we cannot allow anger to be the force of our communication. I tell people that if they need to remove themselves from a situation due to the amount of anger involved, then do it because words spoken in anger breed regret. When a person is speaking from heightened emotions, they will begin to speak words that they will soon regret. Many people are so quick to speak from a place of heightened emotions that they add extra animosity on the other person and the relationship begins to separate even more.

Many people are so anxious to get their point across that they miss out on actually listening to what the other person has to say. Listen in order to understand what is being said – don't just wait for the other person to finish. When someone is speaking with someone do you automatically formulate what you are going to say back or do you listen for understanding? James 1: 19-20 is encouraging us to hear beyond what is just being said. We have to be able to hear through not just our ears, but our eyes as well – look at body language, mood, tension, etc.

Take the time to hear and be slow to speak.

Before we speak, we have to take the time to make sure that our heart is in the right place. This is why James commands us to pump the brakes before opening our mouths, especially if there is the potential for anger. In addition to being quick to hear and slow to speak, we also have to be slow to anger. If I follow the process of communication in this verse then my anger will be diluted in my communication. Many people speak from a place of bitterness. As I am writing this, we are in the middle of the election season. Have you watched the debates? Neither candidate is seeking to understand the other, all they want to do is get their point across and discredit the other. It is pivotal that we do not let bitterness sit in our heart – whatever we allow to sit in our heart long enough will eventually manifest in what we say. The devil and his demons know that the best way to disconnect two people who love each other is for them to harbor destructive emotions, such as bitterness, resentment, and un-forgiveness. If these emotions are harbored and not dealt with, they will result in contentious communication and a lot of regret. The tone of the conversation will be harsh and words will be spoken out of anger. Even if the individual is right, the angry tone of the conversation will result in more animosity and further separate the two.

How many relationships are bruised today because of words that were never meant to be said? Anger gives hollow words weight – meaning what you say may not be that significant but because it carries a tone of anger, it can do extra damage that didn't need to be done. Nothing good happens from anger or heightened emotions. Imagine if we practiced what Proverbs 15:1 says: 'a soft answer turns away wrath, but a harsh word stirs up anger.' How many relationships could have been saved by following this command? How many arguments could be quenched with a soft answer? When you take the time to listen and develop compassion for the other person, you will begin to really understand them and can avoid heartache in relationships. Remember, tone is everything in communication.

Let's talk about constructive communication.

The two scriptures we are going to use to address constructive communication are as follows: Ephesians 4:29 and Colossians 4:6. Ephesians 4:29 states, 'let no corrupting thought come out of your mouth, but only such as good for building up as fits the occasion that it may give grace to those who hear.' It is imperative that we guard what we say. Any conversation that is carnal isn't constructive. Constructive communication seeks to build, uplift, and has a purpose. Anything corrupt has no purpose, whether a simple idea or a philosophy, it doesn't benefit anyone. We have to make sure that we don't consume anything in our heart that will manifest itself in corrupt speech. Our speech is a direct reflection of our heart – corrupt heart, corrupt speech, every time. Proverbs states that our heart is the wellspring of life, therefore we must constantly watch over our heart to make sure that our speech is edifying. This means purging our hearts of corruptness and evil, constantly washing it with the word of God, through community, accountability, and surrounding ourselves with good influences.

In order for corrupt speech to not come out of my mouth, I have to make sure that I produce another form of speech that does three different things: builds up, fits the occasion, and gives grace to those who hear. Everything that comes out of our mouths must be seasoned with the motive of building up. Anytime I speak with someone, my objective is to listen for buzz words so that I can discern exactly what they are going through. These words give me connection points in my conversations, they let me know if people are depressed or aren't in good spirits. Once I know those things, I will find ways to build them up and to give them motivation to keep going. This is exactly why I love speech – it is incredibly powerful. Just by listening intently and speaking to someone's soul, you can spark a revolution inside of them. Your words can unlock potential, your words can motivate them to accomplish things that they never dreamed of. Keep in mind that your communication is only as good as your hearing. You must be slow to speak, slow to anger, and quick to hear – then you can begin infusing hope to everyone you come in contact with.

Constructive communication isn't just conversation that builds up and enlightens - it also corrects. Correction is focused on helping you identify areas in which you can develop. Sometimes this means tearing down old ideas, philosophies, and ideologies and building something brand new in their place. Many people do not like tough love but there are times when we all have to be pushed and torn down in order to grow. There will be times where you have to speak truth into people's lives even though they do not want to hear it. They may feel like you are tearing them down even though that isn't your intent. There is power in the word 'no', power in the words, 'I shouldn't', power in the words, 'I think you should change here or there.' There is power in those words because when you are in a community and receiving healthy criticism from other believers, you are being bettered. Please understand that everything must be presented in grace; make sure that your tone isn't sharp or demeaning, but loving. There are two things that I share with someone when I give them constructive criticism: the importance of a beam vs. a speck and what I like to call the "Triple C Sandwich": cheer, critique, cheer.

Speck vs. Beam

Scripture implores us to take the beam out of my eye so that we will be able to clearly see the speck in the other's eye. This means that you must look at your heart prior to criticizing someone else. Ask yourself what could be hindering you from seeing this situation the right way. Make sure you do not approach them with an attitude of pride, arrogance, or ego. Let grace and mercy lead you in your conversation with them and make sure that you have removed the beam in your eye to see the speck in theirs.

Triple C Sandwich

Prior to correcting someone, it is imperative that you tell the individual what they are doing well. Once you do this, you are now ready to give a constructive criticism. Make sure that you give them another cheer after this so they don't walk away discouraged. Emphasize that you are doing this from a place of love and truth and is meant to help them.

The next is, it has to fit the occasion.

Nothing is worse than when someone speaks words that do not fit the occasion. Discernment is key in conversation because if you are led by the Sprit, your words will always fit the occasion. Many people do not speak what fits the occasion because they don't take the time to discern what is really going on. When you take the time to discern the situation, you may realize that now isn't the time to quote Scripture or uplift; it may just be time to listen and understand, or to even weep with them. One verse that is applicable to this situation is Romans 12:15: 'rejoice with those who rejoice and weep with those who weep." When a person is rejoicing, we need to participate in that with them, let them have their moment. Even if there is something that we are angry at, we need to rejoice because that fits the occasion. The same is true of weeping. We aren't told to try to fix whatever is wrong with that other person – simply empathize with them and weep alongside.

It will give grace to those who hear.

When a person is willing to humble themselves and focus on each person they come across, they are giving out grace. Many people are living life without being given grace. We are quick to judge and tear down because we are insecure. We are not secure in Christ and what he did for us. We don't like it when someone rejoices because we are jealous. We don't take time to sit down with someone to help them walk through something – instead we distance ourselves. When we do these things, we aren't giving grace to people. Make sure, no matter your age or marital status, that you are building up others around you constantly. Make sure you build up your loved ones, sons, daughters, friends, parents. Listen intently and use discernment to fit your words to their occasion and give them the grace they desperately crave.

Psalm 141:3 is another great scripture concerning communication. It says, "set a guard oh Lord over my mouth, keep watch over the door of my lips.' This scripture is powerful because it reminds us that we aren't great communicators in our own strength – we have to ask God to help us guard our words. Every time we say something that isn't good, we have to ask the Holy Sprit to correct us. We have to ask God to set a guard over the door of our mouth. We have to make sure that God is at every entrance, every doorpost, our ear-gates, eye-gates, everything. When God is the gate-keeper of our life, it allows us to be open to him convicting us when we are wrong. God has given us a spirit of discernment when it comes to our words. I always tell people to mull over every word that they speak. Make sure you audit, chew, observe, and look through every word before you speak it. Just because you feel like saying something, doesn't mean that you need to say it. We have to allow our communication to be committed to God, because if it isn't, you will have a loose mouth in your relationships, marriage, around your kids, at work etc. You hear people make excuses for saying things just because they "feel" like it. You have to remember that feelings aren't always factual. Take a step back to see if your feelings line up with reality and don't allow them to cloud your judgment and speak non-constructive words.

Lastly, in order for our communication to be powerful and effective, it has to be concise. By definition, concise means "restricted" or "limited". There are two scriptures that deal with clear and concise communication: Proverbs 10:19 and 18:13. Proverbs 10:19 reads, "When words are many, transgression is not lacking." When a person is loose with their words, they lack restraint. When we don't use concise communication, we get ourselves in trouble. There are those of us who have lost relationships due to speaking too much. Many are unaware, that voluminous words can cause trouble. There can be words of violence, frustration, and sin. That's why the Bible says in Proverbs 19 that whoever restrains his lips is prudent. Even if you know for a fact that you are correct in a given situation, the prudent thing to do may be to say nothing. Let God give you the discernment to know what to say. I cannot emphasize enough – let God lead you in conversation so that you can be clear and concise with your words.

Proverbs 18:13 also gives us good insight. It says, "If one gives an answer before he hears, it is to his folly and shame." You have to make sure that you hear before you answer, or else you will look unwise. Are you letting your words be led by the wisdom of God or wishful thinking? Are you allowing your words to be led by wonder and curiosity or are you strong enough in Christ to let your words be concise? In order for us to be effective communicators, our communication must be calm, constructive, committed, and concise.

Group Questions:

Why is communication so important?

Why is it wrong to assume?

Why is it important for us to act from clarity?

In what ways could you improve in making your communication calm, constructive, committed and concise? Feel free to discuss these points with a friend or in a group!

Chapter 10 – *Policies and Procedures*

Many of us have open borders but few of us have boundaries. We let people in who simply do not belong. It is very important for us to run our lives like a Fortune 500 company. The following is a list of things that a Fortune 500 company must consider when making decisions: Policies and procedures, requirements and benefits, the hiring and firing of employees, general and limiting information, branding and marketing, general and limited access.

Policies and Procedures

Policies define boundaries and procedures make sure that the boundaries are kept. It is very important for you and I to have policies and procedures so that we know what defines us and what we let into our lives. Once we know the policies we must have procedures in place to make sure that those policies are kept. There are certain policies that you must have before engaging with family, friends, and a future spouse. Many of us have no policies, therefore we allow our lives to be unguarded. Or if we do have policies, we do not have procedures to enforce those policies and to stay committed to them. It's sad when a woman has a policy of abstinence but the moment that she gets lonely she allows a man to come into her life and have sex with her. She failed to have a procedure in place to protect that policy. What she doesn't realize is that man and no other man will respect that policy again. Or if a man has a policy of not watching porn but no procedure in place to uphold it, he will fall right back into watching pornography.

A good company communicates their policies clearly and makes sure that they have procedures in place to uphold those policies. When there are no policies and procedures there will always be compromise. Ask yourself today what your policies and procedures are. What are your limits, what are your standards, what are your beliefs? If you haven't defined these and have no procedures in place to uphold them, then you will eventually compromise. Please understand that the establishment of policies is only half of the battle. You have to have step-by-step procedures in place so that when there is a challenge to the policy, that policy will stand. For example, if you are going to wait until you are married to have sex, make sure that you have procedures in place to protect that policy.

Requirements and benefits are another thing that good companies must have in place. No company will allow anyone to have access to their medical or retirement benefits, unless they meet the requirements of the company. Many people are giving others access to their benefits without first seeing if they meet their requirements. This is especially true of insecure people. They will allow others to take advantage of them and give them access to things they shouldn't – sex, their mind, heart, etc. I tell people that before you release your benefits you must establish requirements. Before you allow people to inquire about your requirements, you have to ask for a resume. You have to ask people about their history – how many relationships have they had, why did they end, what did you learn from them? Why should you hire them into your life?

Anything that is allowed easy access to its value is cheapened. This is the difference between something that is available on a shelf versus something that is available in a vault. If it's available on a shelf then it is easy to access; if it is in a vault, I have to meet certain requirements to get access. As believers it is imperative that we understand that God has requirements of us. We were bought with a price and with that purchase comes a new order and a new level of living. His requirements now become our requirements and we discover these requirements through prayer and His Word. If you are a believer, you are no longer your own. You do not establish your requirements – God does. You will not know what His requirements are if you do not pray and read His word. This is the only way that you will find out what your purpose is.

If you don't know what God's intentions are for you, you will establish all kinds of requirements that give the wrong people access to you. For instance, if you are a single woman what are your requirements? If you don't have any, then you will only look for a handsome man, not a godly man. Even if he is a Christian, do you see any fruit? You can't just make a judgment based on Christian rituals – anybody can hold their hand up in the air during a service and attend church every week. You need to dive deeper – how does he treat his mother? Does He seek God's will in everything that he does? We get so caught up in a person who looks the part only and isn't the real deal. You can't know if a person is the real thing until you observe he/she for a period of time. Even then you have to ask the Holy Spirit for discernment. There is a difference between your feelings and God's discernment. Discernment is not in your feelings, it is in your spirit. Your feelings have the potential to lead you in the wrong direction because your feelings are based on what you focus on. If you focus on attraction, your feelings will follow. However, if you allow discernment to lead you, you will see beyond just the attraction. You will focus on the heart instead.

I tell people, no ring no fling, no fruit, no roots, no proven fruit, no need to anchor roots. The Bible talks about observing fruit constantly – "You will know them by their fruit." Or to put it another way, you will know them by what they bare, not how they are packaged. If you keep looking at their package and how they adorn themselves, you will constantly fall into traps. This happens all of the time in relationships – there is sizzle but no substance. To sum up, before you release your benefits, establish your requirements; before establishing requirements, look at the resumes. If their resume doesn't meet God's requirements, then you need to remove their resume from the pile.

Another good trait of a Fortune 500 company is that they know whom to hire and fire. In our relationships, we have to learn how to hire and be strong enough to fire people who don't meet our standards. Not everyone who is connected to us needs to be with us for the whole journey. Many of us get both the hiring and firing wrong. We hire the wrong people and fire the right people. The only way to get the hiring and firing of people correct is to be constantly led by the Spirit. The good news is that there is a system in place that has been given to us by God – his Holy Spirit. We not only need for him to lead and guide us into all truth, we have to ask him to guide us to who we allow into our lives. We have to look at our lives like a business. When you look around your business, are you loyal to a fault to people in your life? Loyalty can ruin your legacy. If you are too loyal, you will allow leeches into your life. You have to be able to draw the line with some people and release them from your life. You can even love that person but they may not be right for this phase of life. They may be good as aunts, uncles, cousins, etc. but be bad for business and ministry. You cannot cut people out completely, but certain ones can no longer be invested in certain phases of your life.

Another thing that makes a good company great is that they know how to distinguish between general information and limited information. They know which things to keep private and which things to make public. For example, companies have general information on their website – how they were formed, what their purpose is, etc. However, there is other information that they keep private – acquisition strategies, financial information, etc. If this information falls into the wrong hands, it will give the competition an advantage. When it comes to giving up intimate personal information, we need to practice the same caution. We need to know what to disclose and what not to. When information is limited, it can be more valuable. Leave room for imagination – attraction rather than promotion.

Branding and Marketing

Successful businesses have effective branding and marketing strategies. They make sure that they can deliver what they advertise. I tell people to make sure that they only advertise what they have in stock. Before you market yourself to the opposite sex, you have to define what your brand is. You also have to ask yourself how people will view you. This applies to both single and married life. What is unique about you? Do you have a personal mission statement? Are you too focused on trying to copy someone else's brand? Many of us are marketing ourselves as something that we are not. This comes out in what we say and how we dress. If a person is dressing immodestly, you know that they are advertising lust. You cannot get angry at someone who simply wants access to what you are advertising. By dressing this way, your actions speak louder than your words. You have to ask yourself how you are going to market yourself from this day forward. Take a minute to define your brand and figure out what makes you unique. Whatever you market, will determine who buys. We have to make sure that we understand the difference between supply and demand. Just because someone demands something of you doesn't mean that you should supply it.

General Access and Limited Access

Great companies know the difference between general access and limited access. For example, retail stores like Wal-Mart or Target, give general access to people. You are able to shop in the store and use their restrooms. However, those companies have corporate facilities that not everyone has access to. You have to know the distinction between the two. What kind of access do you give? You have to know the "corporate" you and the "consumer" you. Not everyone is meant to consume you on every level. You have to know boundaries – who you are talking to, why you are talking to them, and what you are saying. If you give everyone access, they may hinder what God wants for you to do. There are certain aspects of my life where I give everyone who I come into contact with at least 15 to 30 seconds of my time. Depending on the person or the information, that time may increase. When it comes to family – spouse, parents, mother, I give unlimited access. You have to limit access so that you have enough time for you, God, and to produce what He has gifted you with. Right now people can consume me in a number of different ways: YouTube, Facebook, Twitter, Periscope – but they cannot consume my life. If I allow everyone into my life who access me on my various platforms, I will be sucked dry. I try to surround myself with people who are assets that will drive me forward.

Questions and Exercises

I want you to take some time and develop your Fortune 500 Company. Below are some exercises to help you develop a successful business (life) feel free to do this alone or with a group.

Policies and Procedures:

I want you to define below your policies and your procedures. I want you to utilizes the boxes below to define your commitments and how you plan to uphold them.

What will you allow in your life	What will you not allow in your life
What are you committed to?	What are you not going to be committed to?

Define your standards and how you plan to keep them. "I will and I will not"

Define your limits and how you plan to protect them.

Define your beliefs and how you plan to sustain them.

What do you value and how do you plan to maintain their value?

Requirements and Benefits + Hiring and Firing

I want you to write down below your Godly requirements and your benefits or in other words what makes you beneficial to someone else. I want you to utilizes the boxes below to develop your requirements and your benefits package.

What does God require from you as a person?

Utilize the list above to develop your new requirements.

List below your benefits and why they need to be guarded?

Who are the people receiving benefits from you right now?	Do these individuals match your requirements? (yes or no)
• • • • •	• • • • •

If yes, why do they still deserve access to your benefits and if no why do they need to be cut-off?	

What kind of people would you like to hire into your life?	Who right now needs to be fired out of your life; or out of a certain phase of your life?

General Info and Limited Info + General Access and Limited Access

I want you to write down below the info that needs to be private and the info that's ok to be public. Remember not everyone needs to know everything about you.

Private Info about you	Public Info about you
Why should the info above stay private?	**Why is it ok for the info above to be public?**
Who is on your corporate team? In other words, who should have full access.	**Who or what group of people just need limited access to you?**

Branding and Marketing

I want you to utilize the boxes below to develop your Brand. Feel free to use another sheet of paper.

How do you think people view you?	How would you like to be viewed?
Do the two above contradict? If so what changes need to be made?	What would you like to be drawn to you? And what needs to be in your life now to draw these things

What is your mission statement: (**Coach Josh**: My mission is to build people, to build relationships and to build communities) List below the two or three things you want to fix or to help. My mission is to:

11

Walking with God demands wisdom, zeal, poise, and persistence. We all have a call from God and this call requires us to put into practice those traits. This call demands zeal and enthusiastic diligence. However, zeal alone leads a person nowhere; wisdom must balance zeal. By definition, zeal means "enthusiastic diligence." This means that we have an enthusiastic, forceful, powerful, and momentous energy that leads to accomplishing our God-given task. If a person has zeal but no wisdom to guard it, then that zeal will cause them to plummet. Zeal without wisdom leads to destruction. Zeal may be productive in the beginning but it will fizzle eventually without wisdom to taper it.

A lot of people have a zeal for business, marriage, and ministry but they haven't allowed themselves to mature under wisdom's umbrella. Without wisdom, we will not discern the will of God because He governs everything based upon patience and wisdom. These two work together to ensure God's perfect timing. A lot of people want to "just do it" but lack the necessary preparation and plans to execute on those things.

Aspects of Wisdom

There are three aspects to wisdom: Price, fruit, and acts. Proverbs 3:13-18 states, "Blessed is the one who finds wisdom and the one who gets understanding, for the gain from her is better than gain from silver, and her profit better than gold. She is more precious than jewels and nothing you desire can compare with her. Long life is her right hand and left hand are riches and honor. Her ways are ways of pleasantness and all her paths are peace. She is a tree of life to those who laid hold of her, those who hold her fast are called blessed." This text compares wisdom to a woman because of her ability to nurture. Wisdom is a nurturer, a caretaker, and a place of understanding. When you dwell with wisdom you are nurtured and cared for. Solomon compares wisdom to precious jewels, silver, and gold. The richest man that ever walked the face of the earth testifies that wisdom is worth more than an infinite amount of money.

Wisdom gives you exuberance and a glow. The Bible talks about how her ways are pleasant and her paths are peace. If you want to have a peaceful life, you have to dwell with wisdom. A lot of people are married and wealthy due to their zeal, but only wisdom will make those things last. Wisdom gives you the ability to take a step back and ponder not just your path but all of the small nuances that go into making a solid decision. It allows you to not just become successful but sustain that success. I would rather be successful twenty years from now then gain success in two years and lose everything due to a lack of wisdom. The gains from acquiring wisdom are numerous – not just external profits but internal security and peace as well. She will guard you. She will lead you down God's path which dovetails with His will. Finally, remember that God's wisdom will never endorse your will, only His.

Next are the fruits of wisdom. James 3:13-18 says, "Who is wise and understanding among you? By his good conduct let him show his works in the meekness of wisdom. But if you have bitter jealousy and selfish ambitions in your hearts do not boast and be false to the truth. This is not the wisdom that comes from above but it's earthly, unspiritual, and demonic. For where jealousy and selfish ambition exists there will be disorder and every vile practice. But the wisdom from above is first pure then peaceable, gentle, open to reason, full of mercy and good fruits, impartial and sincere. And a harvest of righteousness is sown and peace by those who make it." Wisdom has fruits too. There are two types of wisdom – God's wisdom and the world's wisdom. At its core, the world's wisdom is jealous and selfish. These two traits fuel people to acquire wealth and a certain way of life. They may not say it out loud, but their actions indicate that jealousy is the driving force behind what they do. Jealous people are more consumed about what other people have versus how they went and got it. I always tell people that your greatest competitor is the you from yesterday. Jealous people do not have the character to handle the things that they want.

Selfish Ambition.

Most of our ambitions are self-centered and do not center around advancing the Kingdom of God or helping other people. Our desire is to exalt ourselves and see just how much we can get. James talks about what happens when there is selfish ambition – disorder and envy. Selfish ambition and jealousy will cause you to cut corners and get to the, "I do" too quickly no matter what it is.

Every Vile Practice

When a person is jealous, all of their practices are evil at the core because they are doing everything out of self-centeredness. For many of us, the only reason we are on the path that we are, is not because of joy, but because of selfishness. Are you self-centered or people-centered? You have to ask yourself these questions because these character traits are not easily found in the fruit; they are found in the vine. When you look at your heart, check to make sure that the vine is good and that your wisdom is pure. The Bible lets us know that we have to make sure our wisdom is pure and is from above. Is your wisdom pure, peaceable, gentle, open to reason, and full of mercy? Does my wisdom have good fruit? Is it impartial and sincere? If this doesn't describe your wisdom then your zeal is not protected from the right kind of wisdom.

Verse 17 states, "But the wisdom from above is first pure." The word "pure" means without contaminants, intrusion, or mixture. Wisdom that comes from above will always be pure. The pureness must come from a place and this place is the person of God. Is the wisdom you are receiving from God? You will know for certain if it parallels God's Word. Many people want God to have a rhema word, but He won't give a rhema until you are committed to his written word. Many people want more revelation from God but they don't want to take the time to study His word to give them context on what they might receive. Why would God give you a rhema word when He knows that you aren't willing to build a solid foundation by first understanding his written word? We must filter everything we do and say through Scripture so that we can distinguish between wisdom that is from God and wisdom that is from the World.

Next, wisdom is peaceable. If it is reckless, antagonistic, envious or disruptive, it didn't come from God; His wisdom is always peaceable. God promises to give us the peace that passes understanding (Phillipians 4:7). His presence will come with peace. If you want to find out where you stand in His will, ask yourself what kind of peace you have right now. If there is turmoil and chaos inside of you, that is a clue that you need to sit down and evaluate. God is not a harsh God – He knows the exact amount of gentleness and toughness that you need to understand Him. His wisdom always comes gently so that you can receive it.

His wisdom is open to reason. He isn't just going to give you a word that hasn't been proven. He is anchored in integrity and truth. He won't give you anything that doesn't have a trail of truth to it because truth gives you peace, it will set you free (John 8:32). God's wisdom is always reasonable; when it's time to present it, others will be able to reason through it and find it's truth. He wants you to ask questions about what He gives you because that shows a level of maturity. Most people don't ask questions when things are presented, but God wants you to investigate and chew on everything that He presents to you.

This verse of Scripture also says that His wisdom is full of mercy and good fruit. Did you know that we don't even have the right to even hear God's wisdom? Since we are sinners by default, God's wisdom doesn't come naturally to us – He has to give it to us. Despite our fallen state, God is going to give us wisdom through mercy that is infused with His love. The best way to test whether something has been given to you by God is to discover what comes behind it. If you want to know for a fact whether you are on the right path, ask what type of fruit is on this tree. The Bible says that the blessing of the Lord adds no sorrow (Proverbs 10:22) and that everything good comes down from the father of lights (James 1:17). The world's wisdom will always lead you to sorrow because it always leads you away from God. If you are being led by God's wisdom, you will always bear good fruit. Many people get upset with "good fruit" because they think that it should be success, money, women, men, marriage – all tangible things. What happens is that they begin to follow God but when those tangible fruits don't appear, they think that the wisdom they are obtaining isn't from God. I personally believe that God bares you fruit internally before he bares you fruit externally.

God's wisdom isn't partial – He doesn't play favorites. His wisdom has no respect of persons or ages. The Kingdom of God has no classes, no hierarchy, and no levels. Everyone is equal under the blood of Christ. Anyone can go before God and ask for wisdom, whether you have been a Christian for 40 years or you just got saved yesterday. Christ's death on the cross gave us the access to ask God for wisdom. All we have to do is ask for it in humility. We have to know that we lack it and only God can give it to us.

The Acts of Wisdom

Ephesians 5:15-17 says, "Look carefully then how you walk; not as unwise but as wise. Making the best use of the time because the days are evil. Therefore do not be foolish but understand what the will of God is." In order for us to perform acts of wisdom, we must understand what God's will is. It is pivotal that we walk in acts of wisdom. One act of wisdom is to look carefully, observe, and process through things. This requires patience. Ephesians talks about these being the "last days" so we have to make sure that we act with wisdom. You have to be able to think through every move and every step you take. There are consequences to every choice - that is why you need to proceed with discipline, instruction, and caution. Process every step you take.

Being led by God.

In order to be led by God you have to be sensitive, secure, and steady. In order to be led by God you have to be sensitive. You cannot allow your spirit-man to be chaotic; it has to be still. You have to trust. In order for you to be sensitive toward someone you have to trust him or her. The more you trust God, the more sensitive you become to Him. The more you engage with God and journal about your experiences with Him, the more sensitive you will become. God proves his faithfulness towards us visually and audibly. When we see it visually and hear it audibly and see that God is involved in the details of our lives, it makes us trust Him even more. The more that I trust, the more sensitive I become; the more sensitive I am, the more I am led. If you trust a person; you are more likely to follow them. You will follow their instructions whether it makes sense or not

Security

In order to be led by God you have to be secure in who you are in Him, and what His word says about life. Many people are nervous and afraid about where God is leading them. In order for you to get to that place, you have to be secure in Him first. If you are insecure, you will be holding His hand and then eventually letting it go. Take comfort though. Even giants of the faith like Moses went through this. He was insecure about what to tell Pharaoh about who sent him; he was insecure about this stuttering problem. We all go through it, but eventually we have to let go and let God do His thing. God doesn't care about your defects or your inadequacies. He doesn't qualify the qualified - he qualifies the unqualified. Your security shouldn't be in any college degrees or certifications that you have or don't have. There is another hindrance to following God – when an individual is too secure. When people are secure based upon their accomplishments and/or how much they know, they lack the necessary humility to follow God. Therefore, if God leads them to a more humble road they don't want to leave their secure place to follow in potential uncertainty. God will always lead you into places that aren't secure, because that is the only way to develop faith. He will lead you into places that are uncomfortable and stretch you in order to demonstrate His power and faithfulness.

A lot of people reading this book are insecure in their abilities. You may be secure in God's ability, but you're not secure in your ability. You can do all things through Christ who strengthens you. 'All things' doesn't mean everything, but it does mean everything as it pertains to you. You can do whatever God has called you to do at a high level. God has predestined you for great things that will surpass your own intellect. Yes, you may not be famous but you can be the best thing since sliced bread to your son and daughter. If you aren't secure in your ability, then you won't be secure in God's perception of you.

Steady

The next thing that you have to learn is how to be steady. Steady means being consistent. Steadiness means that you are going to show up every day for school, practice, work, whatever it is that you are involved in. If you play basketball, it may mean taking 100 free throws. You are guaranteed to miss every shot you don't take. I have to be consistent. I have to make sure that I am obedient, that I show up. However, I won't be steady if I'm not sensitive and if I'm not secure. Your steadiness is predicated on your sensitivity towards God. He wants a faithful person to follow Him. If you're not faithful in the small things, you won't be faithful in the big things. You cannot be faithful without showing up on a consistent basis. Remember these three things because they are linked together: In order to be led you have to be secure, sensitive, and steady. When you have these traits your destination is guaranteed.

What did you learn from this chapter and what changes do you need to make when it comes to your zeal?

12

Contrary to popular belief, God demands that we work hard. People come into Christianity thinking that God owes them something. When a person has this mentality, they end up nowhere. They think that all they have to do is a little and God will do all of the heavy lifting. Then they wonder why they aren't having success. They fail to realize that the reason why people are successful is because they work hard. I wish there was more to it, but that is how God designed it to work. He wants us to develop a great work ethic. He cares about this, because He cares about our excellence, which is demonstrated by the quality of our work. Many people work hard but their hard work is not quality.

The opposite of diligence and hard work is laziness and procrastination. The prudent are diligent and hard-working and the sluggard is lazy and procrastinates.

The sluggard does these 5 things: Craves, slacks off, lacks sense, seeks, and loves to sleep.

Craves

The sluggard craves - Proverbs 13:4 says 'The soul of the sluggard craves and gives nothing while the soul of the diligent is richly supplied.' A sluggard craves for things they are not willing to work for. When someone craves and gets nothing, they have self-pity and make excuses. Your focus, diligence, and your discipline should outlast your cravings. When a person is not willing to endure and persevere to obtain their craving; they get nothing. Wouldn't you find that person annoying if they talked about craving a cup of coffee yet were too lazy to get it? People don't want to hear your cravings; they want to see if you're willing to go get it. The ultimate craving we should have is to hunger and thirst after righteousness. When we hunger and thirst after righteousness, our craving will not be met until we meet Him. The craving that was set before Jesus helped him endure the cross. He is essentially saying to us, "Now I want to be the craving set before you. I want to be the joy set before you so that you will come after me until you complete it." If you crave something but aren't willing to go complete it then chances are you will end up empty-handed. The sluggard craves and gets nothing because they don't have enough endurance to complete it.

Slacks

The sluggard slacks. The Bible says in Proverbs 18:9 'Whoever is slacking his work is a brother to him who destroys.' A person who doesn't finish ends up being in the company of those who destroy. A lot of the people who are committing crimes are people who never started something or never completed anything. For example, if you don't complete school and get your degree and the degree helps you get to a certain destination, then you become filled with inadequacies and insecurities. Recently riots broke out in Charlotte. The reason why I wasn't down there breaking windows and screaming at the top of my lungs is because I'm trying to finish my work. The rioters are people who had idle time. What happens when you have idle time? Idle time leads to an idle mind, an idle mind leads to idle hands, and idle hands lead to an idle life. When a person is idle, they fulfil the desires of their idleness. They do stupid things and just make situations worse. Whoever is slack in his work, will destroy. The sluggard starts but never finishes. When you are focused, you will achieve.

Lacks sense

Proverbs 24:30-34 says "I pass by the feet of a sluggard, by the vineyard of a man lacking sense. And behold, it was all overgrown with thorns, the ground was covered with nettles and its stone walls were broken down. Then I saw and considered it, I looked and received instruction. A little sleep, a little slumber, a little folding of the hands to rest and poverty will come upon on you like a robber and want like an armed man." The sluggard lacks common sense. Common sense enables you to do things the right way. Unfortunately, common sense is not so common these days. People are intellectually smart but have lost the basics of common sense. Common sense says not to buy a house unless you can afford it; don't take a job if it doesn't pay enough, and don't marry someone unless you are certain. However, the sluggard doesn't think things through. He wants these things but it never works out. Lacking sense says 'I want it but I don't understand it.'

In life, sometimes the best instruction is to look at other people's destruction and the best insight is to look at somebody else's lack of sight. Observe other people's destruction so that you can gain instruction. Proverbs 24:33 says, 'A little sleep, a little slumber, a little fold of the hand to rest and poverty will come upon that person like a robber and want like an armed man.' Poverty and want will grab you if you're not focused. Want will destroy you if you're not willing to go and get the task completed; it is our responsibility to do this. Proverbs is a treasure trove of common sense. Study it and put into practice it's teachings and you will never lack sense.

Seeks

Proverbs 20:4 says "The sluggard does not plow in the autumn. He will seek at harvest and have nothing." The sluggard seeks but never finishes and he does not plow in autumn. We would consider a person a fool that has a field and doesn't plow in autumn and then expects a harvest. We would also consider that person to be a fool for getting mad at God for not bringing the harvest. He isn't following God's principle of sowing and reaping. He needs to plant the seed and tend it, then harvest will have come. Before you seek a return you first have to make an investment; a sluggard seeks with no investment. They seek a harvest but they didn't even plant. Many people want the harvest off of what you planted. Do not allow people in your life to reap a harvest if they weren't there for you when you planted the seeds. The only people that should reap from your harvest are your children and the people God leads you to help. Nobody else should reap from what you've sown because whatever a person receives without toil will damage them. I would rather make a million dollars one dollar at a time than all at once.

Sleep

Proverbs 19:15 says "Slothfulness casts into a deep sleep, and an idle person will suffer hunger." If you are around a person who loves sleeping, playing video games, and having leisure time but does not love to work, that person is a sluggard. Slothfulness casts into a deep sleep. Deep sleep is always initiated by slothfulness. Slothfulness says 'I do things poorly, I do things half way, I never do things the correct way.' When a person wants to reap big things from slothfulness they get insecure and make excuses. They think that they aren't good at anything. The reason why they aren't good at anything is because they are not willing to work at it. In order to be good at something, you have to work at it. You have to be willing to master it. A lot of us are slothful in a lot of things but aren't masters of anything.

Let's talk about what the prudent does. The prudent doesn't love sleep, works unto the Lord, owns, profits, and makes the best use of the time.

The prudent doesn't love sleep.' The Bible says in Proverbs 20:13, "Love not sleep lest you come to poverty. Open your eyes and you will have plenty of bread. Sleep is a resource, not the source. We need sleep but can't be consumed by it. The reason why many people are poor or not successful when it comes to their business, marriage, or ministry is because they love sleep. This doesn't mean simply going to bed, it means they want comfort all of the time. These people are not able to see, that's why the Bible says 'open your eyes and you will have plenty of bread.' The prudent opens their eyes, they don't love sleep. They keep their eyes open for the bulk of the day. Their eyes aren't open just for the bulk of the day but the bulk of their lives. You don't work with your eyes closed, do you? You work with your eyes open. When you work with your eyes open you get the work done and earn your wage. If your eyes are closed most of the day and you're blinded, there won't be any success. The prudent person knows that they need sleep but they don't love sleep. God says He will show your hands how to profit if you keep your eyes open.

The prudent works unto the Lord. Colossians 3:23 says "Whatever you do, work heartily as for the Lord and not for men." The wise person knows that he is here to work for God. He knows that he is employed by the kingdom of heaven. He doesn't work to receive the praise of man but works unto the Lord. God's people who live by this principle outshine a lot of people. Daniel, Shadrach, Meshach, and Abednego outshined a lot of people. So did Joseph and Moses, all because their work was unto the Lord. When you work unto the Lord and are focused, you will have extra energy and be able to outwork people. All we need is the Spirit of God to be energized because we work for the Lord. If you work hard for God you will exceed man's expectations. However, if you work for man's expectations you will rarely meet God's expectations. The prudent works unto to the Lord; not for men.

The prudent follows the leader. John 5:17 says "Jesus answered them: My father is working until now and I am working." Jesus boldly embodied this principle and this is his desire for us as well. Jesus answered them and said 'Since my father is still working, I'm going to continue working.' Your work never ends. Laziness and procrastination should never define any period of your life. Since God is working I need to be working. Jesus took no days off. He took days off to rest, but his rest and sleep were a part of his work. Eating was also a part of his work. He told his disciples after his discussion with the woman at the well, he said 'I eat from food you know not of, because my food is to do the will of God.' When that is your pursuit and you're being nourished by the will of God, you will always have the energy to work. You will *want* to work because you're working with your Father. That's the reason why I write books because if God tells me to do it, I do it.

The prudent owns. Proverbs 12:24 says, "The hand of the diligent will rule while the slothful will be put to forced labor." The wise person owns their creativity. The prudent person says, "I want to own my ministry, my business, and my life. I'm going to own up to it and I'm going to own it." Powerful. If I own what I have, then I will have the maturity to manage it once I have it. The reason why many of us don't own anything is because we aren't willing to own up. Therefore, the diligent will rule while the slothful will be put to forced labor. How many people are working for someone else because they forfeited their dream? The prudent says, "My dream is either my dream or it's nothing." Will you work for people along the way? Yes, but you won't work for people forever. There is nothing wrong with working for a company because we need workers; but let that be your dream job and where you *want* to be; not where you *have* to be. I'm going to speak to the creators, the entrepreneurs out there. Own your content, whatever it is. Right now I own the publishing of all my books and I own my businesses. Am I successful as far as a millionaire when it comes to the things I own? Not yet, but I have enough barrels out there because I am diligent. Since I own the publishing rights to my books, I get all the royalties; I don't have to split this with anyone because I own it. But owning something requires a lot, it requires us to own up. If you are slothful in your work, you will always be working for somebody else.

The prudent profits. Proverbs 14:23 "In all toil there is profit but mere talk tends only to poverty." Have you ever been around people that talk a big game but never get any fruit from it? In all toil there is profit even if you are only working a minimum wage job. Anytime you work you receive a return. Many people refuse to toil because they want immediate profit. When you want immediate profit, you will only grow frustrated. When it comes to life you have to have the end in mind. Right now I have made 600 videos, written three books, with a fourth on the way. This has taken a lot of work. Have I profited from it yet? No, but one day I will. Profits aren't just external – they are also internal. Through my toil, pain, and trials I have become a better person and a better version of myself. No matter what I do there is a profit. I would rather be quiet and toil privately than talk a big game and have no profit. I will choose to toil privately and reap publicly than to talk publicly and accomplish nothing privately.

The prudent also makes best use of the time. Ephesians 5:15-17 says "Look carefully then how you walk, not as unwise but as wise; making the best use of the time because the days are evil." The prudent knows that the days are evil and that they must make the best use of their time. I have to be motivated since the days are evil; I have to make the best use of my time. I would rather you dedicate five hours to your craft each day than to dedicate five hours watching somebody else succeed. Each and every one of us has an extra five hours a day. The sad thing is that the bulk of us are using those hours to do unproductive. If you dedicate three hours a day to your craft and your personal development, by this time next year you will have more profit than you did before. You may not have more money, but you will have more internal fortitude, understanding, and wisdom.

Questions and Exercise: Character Traits of the Sluggard & Character traits of the Prudent.

I want you to look at both list below and ask yourself the honest question; what traits are found in me? Once you have taken some time to reflect I want you to in the last box to write down the areas you need to improve, how you plan to improve them and/or the areas you have mastered.

Sluggard:	Prudent
• Craves • Slacks off • Lacks sense • Seeks • Loves to sleep	• Doesn't love sleep • Works unto the Lord • Owns • Profits • Makes the best use of the time
Improvements	

13

Resistance builds resilience. In order for me to be resilient I have to embrace resistance. Many people run away the moment they feel resistance instead of running towards it. This type of living leads us to avoid what needs to be addressed. Many people are more focused on avoiding than advancing. Advancement can't happen unless I address the resistance. If I neglect to address this, I will never discover what type of a person I can be. Many people feel that resistance means they are going in the wrong direction but most of the time it means you're going in the right direction. If you're going against the crowd, you're probably going the right way. If you're going with the flow, you're probably flowing in the wrong way. Many people don't know the fruit of resistance. Resistance builds resilience and makes us into stronger people. Resistance is God's way of building us.

There are four things that resistance does. Resistance works for us, produces in us, tests us, and causes us. Life is a marathon, not a sprint. Life is about the full duration, not the quick burst and the quick accomplishments. Since life is a marathon, we need to train like we would for a real marathon. Many people are training for life like a sprinter would —not going on long runs, but short bursts. Instead of conditioning for yourself for the 50 yard-dash, you need to condition yourself for the 26.2 mile run. Imagine the person that trains for one mile but has to run 26.2 - will that person have enough endurance to get to the 26th mile? No. But if a person trains beyond 26.2 miles, they will have plenty of endurance to complete the race. In order for me to get to where I want to go, I have to train miles farther past than what I'm striving for. If you train for life as a sprint and you realize that life is a marathon, you will find yourself gasping for air throughout your life.

Let's talk about resistance working for us. 2 Corinthians 4:17 says "For our light afflictions which is but for a moment worketh for us a far more exceeding and eternal weight of glory." Our resistance works for us; what we once thought was a heavy affliction, was actually the resistance we needed for growth. We will look back and know that resistance was actually working *for* us. It is working for us so that we can achieve an eternal weight of glory that will make us resilient and strong enough to make it to the next life. What resistance is doing to me now is making sure that I'm stronger, wiser, and better than I was before. It gives me a greater weight of glory that spans beyond the temporal and is eternal. When I look back, I know that this affliction which I once thought was heavy was actually light. This is because of our perception now. When you first started lifting weights, you don't start by lifting your heaviest, you start by lifting what you can manage. When you begin to lift what you manage, your body and nervous system begin to build strength. What was once heavy for you is now light. The resistance accomplished this. It is only when you realize that the resistance of the weight was working for you and not against you, that you will embrace it and use it for your benefit.

Resistance also produces in us. Romans 5: 3-4 says "More than that, we rejoice in our sufferings knowing that suffering produces endurance, and endurance produces character, and character produces hope." We get upset with suffering because of what we see it doing on the outside of us. When you look at what suffering is doing outside of you, that's depressing. But when you look at what suffering is doing inside of you, it will produce endurance. You know for a fact that this suffering is producing endurance. Remember the order -suffering produces endurance, endurance produces character, and character gives me hope. The longer I endure, the more my character is shaped. When my character is shaped I get excited because something outside of me is shaping me and it builds my hope. Hope deferred makes the heart sick. This happens because we hope in the wrong things. When you hope in the right things you will embrace suffering because that suffering is going to build hope in you eventually.

Resistance tests us. James 1: 2-4 says "Count it all joy my brothers when you meet trials of various kinds. For you know that the testing of your faith produces patience, and let patience have its full effect that you may be perfect, complete, lacking in nothing." Resistance tests what level you're on. This is why you shouldn't count it as strange, but count it as joy, knowing that this trial is testing and developing you. It's testing my faith and if my faith is not tested, how can I be patient and be long-suffering? Patience must have her full effect so that I can be complete, perfect and lacking in nothing. Resistance lets you know where you are. If I try to lift a heavier weight I will find out how strong I am. I will know what I'm capable of. The test shows us where we are and where we could be and enables us to get there. If you run from resistance you will never know what it's trying to produce in you.

Last but not least - resistance *cause* us. Romans 12:12 says, "Rejoice in hope, be patient in tribulation, be constant in prayer." Resistance causes us to rejoice, to be patient and to be constant. When I know that I am going through resistance I can rejoice in my hope and be patient in tribulation. In order for me to rejoice in the hope that I'm unsure of, and patient in the tribulation that I'm uncomfortable with I have to be in constant prayer when I feel like God is quiet. I have to have the right perception. If I don't see the resistance correctly, I won't rejoice in the hope that the resistance is going to produce in me. If I'm not cautious and I'm not having the right perception, then how can I be patient in tribulation? If I don't have the right perception of resistance, how can I be constant in communication with God? When we have the right perception, resistance produces more out of us than we can ever imagine. Are you allowing the resistance to work for you, to produce in you, to test you, and to cause you? If you're not you're going to fall under it. God is looking for a resilient remnant, not a weak remnant. That's why the church went through so much in the beginning - the real remnant. The real remnant goes through so much right now because God is building them for the latter times. If you are living right now, you are being built for the latter times. If you're afraid of resistance you will divorce quickly, quit easily, and avoid difficulties. People divorce the moment they feel resistance. The resistance can build your marriage - there are lots of people who went through adversity and their marriage became stronger because they didn't quit. When you quit you'll never know how strong your marriage could be. You'll never know what kind of strength you have when it comes to your sexual purity if you don't fight the resistance. I have first-hand knowledge of this - I'm a thirty year old virgin. Have I been perfect? No. However, I am able to tell people, "If I can make it to 30 being a virgin, you can too." If you make excuses, you will never know what you could have executed on.

Questions and Exercise:

I want you to write down below the things you are currently going though and I want you to in each box write down how your current trail could be used to build your resiliency. Remember perception is everything.

Resistances: List them below	
<ul><li></li><li></li><li></li><li></li><li></li><li></li></ul>	
How could the resistances above be working for you?	What could the resistances above be producing in you?
In what ways, could the resistances above be testing you?	What are the resistances above causing you to do?

14

Chapter 14 - Sexual Purity

Sex is a gift from God, but that gift is only safe in a marriage. In order for sex to be holy, the husband and wife must both be completely submitted to God. The Bible warns us not to awaken love before its time (Song of Solomon 2:7). When a person awakens something that they're not mature enough to handle, that thing will be a burden to them. God created sex as a blessing but many of us turn that blessing into a burden. Are you willing to commit to being pure? The reason why many of us are not pure sexually is because we have no self-worth. Insecurities are the number one things in our culture that is keeping us from being mature. Do you love you? Do you care about you? Because you cannot have boundaries around your body if you're not secured within your soul. We have allowed people to engage with us sexually. Either we wanted it for ourselves or we are so burdened with insecurities and low self-esteem that we are too weak to guard ourselves. You are who you are by the pursuit of Christ, not based upon what you want to pursue to satisfy your sexual desires. We have to understand the beauty of sex, but also the dangers of it. Do you care about you? What is your self-worth? What value do you have on you? How much are you worth to yourself? A person who considers themselves worthy and full of value would not allow anyone access to them. Who are you allowing to access your personal space that shouldn't be?

Not everyone should have the ability to touch you because there is power in touch. When you allow someone to touch you it builds up a sexual force in you. Once that happens, you will become a prisoner to that sexual moment. Have you set up boundaries and systems in your life to ensure that you are building your worth? Are you protecting yourself? If you aren't protecting yourself and are insecure then you will allow anyone to access your personal space. This can be physical, spiritual, and emotional. When you allow a person into your personal space physically, luring them through your insecurities, or through lustful desires, then you're setting yourself up for two things: soul-ties and strongholds. You were created to only be soul-tied to your soulmate and to God. A soul-tie is an emotional connection with a person, place, or past experiences. Soul-ties carry over into our day to day lives because our soul is our core, and whatever lies in there flows out. Who or what are you soul-tied to? Many of us are soul-tied to a person that has moved on. We're connected to them but they are not connected to us because we allowed ourselves to blend our souls with them. Sex is the greatest bond between two people because you are both completely exposed physically and emotionally. So that person you've engaged with now has a part of your soul and vice versa. Twenty minutes of pleasure can lead to twenty twenty years of soul-ties.

Sex is the strongest soul-tie but you could also be soul-tied to a past experience, or a person that you've never had sex with. Right now I'm tied to my family and my loved ones. If anything were to happen to them, I would fight to the death for them. The level of your connection will determine the strength of your soul-tie. Your mind and emotions are your core. Whatever occupies the real estate of your mind and heart will dictate how you feel. You got to be very careful who you allow yourself to be tied to. The wrong soul-ties will become strongholds. How many people have strongholds of bitterness, un-forgiveness, and envy? These strongholds build year after year when you do not allow God to untie them. You have to ask God today, "God I need you to untie me from that person. I need you to deliver me from that person." Your body is your temple and your body is precious. The only person we should engage with sexually is the woman or the man that we are with after we say, "I do." Sex isn't safe in any other context. If you don't know God then you will be in a marriage where you are tied to a person from your past.

The reason why many of us find ourselves in sexual situations, is because of this: significant moments lead to significant memories; significant memories lead to significant momentum; significant momentum lead to significant movements, and significant movements lead to significant mistakes. Every one of us can remember a significant moment. We have to be very careful who we allow in our moments. Moments are significant, because whatever happens in a moment sexually turns into a memory. We find ourselves in moments without thinking about the consequences. How many people are suffering years and years of consequences from twenty minutes? Moments turn into monumental burdens. Many people have long-term consequences from short-term moments. You cannot allow your desires to lure you into moments, that will be engrafted in your mind forever as a memory. If you keep allowing people who do not deserve to be in your personal space, you are going to always have that memory in your mind. Many people cannot progress forward because of sexual moments and the memories of those moments. These moments turn into memories which then build into momentum. This builds to anger, lust, and jealousy. The significant moment led to a significant memory that; the significant memory led to momentum; finally, that momentum led to a significant movement. Either you will move recklessly or you will move with resilience. Most people move recklessly - their momentum is not from forgiveness or how God sees them. Their movement is built from a memory that leads them to move. When you move recklessly, you will make mistake after mistake.

I challenge you to be pure sexually. Even if you haven't up to this point, you can be pure again. All you have to do is repent and ask God to heal you from those wounds. You have to build your self-worth because that leads to self-love, which leads to self-care. If you do not know your worth comes from God, you will always end up feeling worthless. Your worth does not come from searching for a spouse or how much money you have. If you know that your worth comes from God, you will have focus. Focus keeps you from finding yourself in someone's bedroom or backseat. Focus says, "I love myself too much to focus on carelessness; I'm going to focus on things that matter. I'm going to focus on God, I'm going to focus on my craft." You may have made mistakes, you may have a chid out of wedlock or an STD, but it's never too late to learn from your experiences. However, if you continue to live recklessly and allow negative momentum to build, you will continually find yourself leaking in all areas.

Sex is too powerful for immature people. Sex is only safe in a marriage where both the husband and the wife are completely submitted to God; no other place is sex safe. Right now I want you to develop a plan to stay sexually pure. I want you to ask yourself how much worth do you see in yourself. Most of us see our worth in terms of "net worth"; but if you view your worth through the lens of God, there is no dollar value. You have to make sure that you're so content with God, so in love with God, so relentless in pursuing your craft that no one has a clearance to get into your personal space. Whoever you allow to touch you sexually can lead you into a significant moment, which leads to memories, momentum and eventually a movement. You do not want to repeat a cycle that God wants you to break. Are you willing to break the strongholds and untie the soul-ties today? I have a video I want you to watch on YouTube, just simply search Joshua Eze and Soul ties. Watch those videos and learn more about how to untie them. And never forget, be too productive to sin.

Exercise and Questions:

How do you truly see you? What do you like and dislike about yourself?		
On a scale from 1-10 how much do you truly love you?	#	
Why this number?		
Who are you currently soul tied too and why?		
Have you truly forgiven yourself and those individuals?	Yes	No

Why is it important to forgive yourself and them?

Why is it important not to be a prisoner of a significant moment?

Journal below your heart to God and ask him to set you free from your soul ties.

Feel free to use the back of this sheet for more space. #Freedom

15

Many people are living life still affected by what happened in their past. They have allowed their wounds to either make them insecure or too secure. When a person is too secure they don't consult God because they are caught up in who they are. The cause of this problem is what we focus on. We are conditioned to be focused on what happened to us instead of focusing on the present moment. Focusing too much on the past causes people to become complacent and envious. They are so consumed with these different things that they never realize what God has for them.

As I mentioned earlier, the reason why many of us don't advance is because we focus on what is ahead of us instead of what's around us. When we look around us at what we do have and behind us at what Christ has done for us, it gives us significance and worth. It also gives us momentum and focus. But when you focus on what happened to you in the past, you will never be able to embrace what you do have and what Christ has done for you. That's why the devil goes to great lengths in attacking us when we were young. The bulk of what's keeping us from progressing is what has happened to us when we were young. The results of our adulthood are predicated to a degree on the wounds of our childhood. Many people still have unhealed wounds from their childhood, and those unhealed wounds are keeping them from progressing in their adulthood. What is still affecting you? What are those unhealed wounds in your life right now that are keeping you from progressing? Wounded people look to all kinds of people and things to heal their soul, but they fail to realize that the only person that can heal their wounds is God. Today, you are either progressing or digressing because of your insecurities. What are you insecure about? What are those things that are keeping you from progressing? What are those things in your childhood that are affecting you mentally right now?

By definition, insecurity is "uncertainty or anxiety about one's self or lack of confidence." Our confidence and our security should be in God. You will always feel uncertain, doubtful and insecure when your identity and your security is not in Him. Whatever you identify with will determine your identity. Whatever you put your insecurity in will determine what secures you. The sad thing is that many of us have identified ourselves with everything but God. Then we find out that none of those things were able to anchor and secure us. Let's apply this to manhood and womanhood. When you identify yourself with the world's definition of manhood and womanhood you have to constantly change. This is because the world's definition of marriage, love, etc. constantly change. God never intended for these things to just be trends – he intended them to be absolute definitions. When you're trendy versus absolute you are always fluctuating identities. You will be up and down and all around because you are caught up in what's trendy. However, when you are caught up on your path and who God wants you to be, you will become legendary. I am not talking about "global legendary" but legendary to your family and friends who need you to be legendary.

Many people are caught up on being copies versus originals. God never created you to be a copy of anything else but his son. When you are a copy of the son, you find your originality. If you copy anything but Jesus, you will find yourself far short of who he has created you to be. If you put your identity in things like money and relationships, you will never be on solid ground. That's why the Bible cautions against what you build your house on. Many people are building their house on sand thinking that that sand will secure them. Sand isn't strong enough to stay intact. When water comes, storms come, when shaking comes, the sand will begin to separate. Everything in life other than Christ will separate. That's why the Bible says build your life not just on any old rock, but on *the* rock, Jesus Christ.

Insecurities cause us to be inactive in the things we are supposed to do and active in the things we aren't supposed to do. You have to be cautious of what you allow to stop you. We were meant to be unstoppable, unmovable, always abounding. We were created to be progressive, to be confident, to be active in the things that God has called us to be. When you identify yourself in everything but God, you drift from the original identity. And when you begin to drift from the original identity, you become insecure because you realize that you're not walking in the path that you're supposed to. You begin to search for things to make you secure. You become active in the things you are not supposed to do versus being active in the things you are supposed to. When you are inactive in your purpose, you begin to lose fruit, impact, and success. I would rather be active in the things that I am supposed to do and make less money than do the wrong things and become a billionaire. God doesn't measure based upon the currency of our culture. He bases everything on the currency of heaven. What are you doing for heaven today? Are you allowing your insecurities to keep you from your purpose?

There is a process that the enemy uses to produce insecurity. There are six "P's in this process: Plan, place, ponder, penetrate, protect, and portray.

Plan

The process of an insecurity begins with a plan. The enemy will use anything that happen to us to develop a plan against us. He and his army observe us. They look at what has happened to you and see how they can develop a plan against you. If you were molested, raped, abused, neglected, or abandoned, they are going to use those unhealed wounds against you. If those wounds are healed, they will try to use something else. They are going to use your perception about the season you are in, what and who is around you, etc. – they will take that information to see what the best way to attack you is. They are not going to develop a plan in areas where you are strongest. They are going to go to the place where you are the weakest. When you are not careful and observant about what's around you or how the past is affecting you, they will pounce. You must counter with discipline.

Once they have developed a plan based on our reactions, they place thoughts in our minds that will grab our attention. They are going to use things that catch your eye. They place these thoughts in the rich soil of your mind and intend to deepen, water and give them sunlight so they can grow. Once they have our undivided attention they will fuel those thoughts and sprinkle them with just enough fact to make us doubtful and confused. Once we ponder on those thoughts long enough, they penetrate deep into our hearts. The amount of time that you spend ruminating on these thoughts will determine their persuasiveness. Be very careful what you allow into your mind and heart. Whatever you allow in your mind will eventually penetrate and root itself in your heart. The Bible says out of the heart flows the issues of life, that as a man thinketh in his heart so is he. Those seeds become strongholds. Once that stronghold is entrenched, they will leave you alone because they know you are too weak to overcome it.

Just as God protects his interests; the enemy protects his interests. The reason why people are not developing in their singleness is because Satan and his demons sow seeds of discontent within them. They want marriage to appear to be the only thing that matters in life if you are single. They want you to believe that being alone for a season is a bad thing. On the other hand, God never wastes a season...ever. God loves the details of your journey – He wants you to enjoy and learn in the journey so that you can appreciate the destination. Satan and his demons want you to waste difficult seasons, especially singleness.

Now let's talk about reversing these layers of insecurity. In order to reverse your insecurities, you must know that God *is* love, God *sent* love, God *uses* love, and God *enables* us to love. **1 John 4:7-21** says, "Beloved, let us love one another for love is from God. Whoever loves has been born of God and knows God. Anyone who does not love does not know God because God is love. In this the love of God was made manifest among us that God sent his only son into the world so that we might live through him; in this is love. Not that we have loved God, but that he loved us and sent his son to be the propitiation for our sins. Beloved, if God so loved us, we also ought to love one another. No one has seen God. If we love one another God abides in us and his love is perfected in us. By this we know that we abide in him and he in us, because he has given us of his spirit and we have seen and testify that the Father has sent his son to be the savior of the world. Whoever confesses that Jesus is the Son of God, God abides in him and he in God. So we have come to know and to believe the love that God has for us. God is love and whoever abides in love abides in God and God abides in him. By this his love perfected with us so that we may have confidence for the day of judgement, because as he is so also are we in this world. There is no fear in love, but perfect love casts out fear. For fear has to do with punishment, and whoever fears has not been perfected in love. We love because he first loved us. If anyone says I love God and hates his brother, he is a liar for he who does not love his brother whom he has seen cannot love God whom he has not seen. And this commandment we have from him whoever loves God must also love his brother."

Verses 7 -8 says "*Beloved, let us love one another for love is from God. Whoever loves has been born of God and knows God. Anyone who does not love does not know God because God is love.*" Before we can eradicate our insecurities, we must know who love is. Love isn't a product or entity - love is a person. Until we know that God is love and also the original definition of love, then we will never love ourselves. Many people in our world today do not love themselves. If you don't love yourself, then it shows that you're not in love with God. When you are in love with God, He will show you how to love yourself and how to love others. When you know that he is love, it doesn't matter what happened or is happening to you. You will be secure in His love and not be moved. Your insecurities will melt away.

When you know that you are loved by God, you won't allow just anyone into your life. Only when you realize this will you be able to remove those layers of insecurities from your life. How many people are insecure toady because they don't think God loves them? God says, "let us love one another for love is from God and whoever loves has been born of God." (1 John 4:7) You have to be born from him. Nobody in this world knows what true love is until you have been reborn. Most people have genuine love for their family, but that love is still imperfect. Parents who have not been born of God overly love their children. The same thing happens with marriage. When a person hasn't been reborn, he or she will have overbearing love for their spouse. When your love has been born of God, it may take a little while to love correctly but over time you will learn how. You will have a stability and the ability to love correctly. However, when you don't know that He is love and your love has not been born of him, you don't know him.

Not only is God love, God sent love. Verses 10 - 15 says "*In this the love of God was made manifest among us that God sent his only son into the world so that we might live through him; in this is love. Not that we have loved God, but that he loved us and sent his son to be the propitiation for our sins. Beloved, if God so loved us, we also ought to love one another. No one has ever seen God. If we love one another God abides in us and his love is perfected in us. By this we know that we abide in him and he in us, because he has given us of his spirit and we have seen and testify that the Father has sent his son to be the savior of the world. Whoever confesses that Jesus is the Son of God, God abides in him and he in God.*" Love has levels. Before I can be born of love, I have to be born again through Christ. When Jesus was sent, love was sent; he said, "my children on earth will not know what love is until their father comes down and see about their needs, until their father becomes like them." Do you know how love was sent? Jesus came down to earth from heaven, where there was no pain, no suffering, no insecurity, and no disease. For centuries, He heard the outcry of his people praying to him. Their outcry was painful but He had a purpose and a plan. He came down in human form in the humblest of places according to Micah 5:2: "But you, O Bethlehem Ephrathah, who are too little to be among the clans of Judah, from you shall come forth for me one who is to be ruler in Israel (Micah 5:2)."

Did you notice that he was a son of a carpenter? God will put you in places that you may have to spend years in before you accomplish your purpose. Jesus was unknown for thirty years. The weight of his cross was 300 pounds and he was a carpenter's son for 30 years; do you see the correlation? He was around the same type of wood that he would die on. He was unknown for 30 years and then appointed by a man, John the Baptist. He knew what it was like to be an unknown. He knew what it was like to submit himself to another man's authority. He knew what it was like to walk amongst the people being famous - his twitter feed was famous. He was known all over the world. His Facebook was strong, his Snapchat, everybody was following him. He knew what it was like to be around people who weren't for him. He walked through this life knowing what it was like to be famous, and knowing what it was like to be alone. In fact, the Bible says that there was a moment when he was in the Garden of Gethsemane that he was so stressed that he actually sweated drops of blood. He was holding the whole weight of the world and its sin. He was betrayed by a man he trusted. He was beaten beyond recognition. His beard was stripped. They made our savior carry his cross. They laid him on the wood, nailed his hands and feet, and pierced his side. Before they pierced his side, Jesus knew what it was like to be abandoned. The Bible reads that the father turned his back on his son. Did you know that Jesus didn't want to do this? He asked God to take his cup from him. The key is that he said, 'not my will but thy will be done.' When you get to a place where you say 'not my will but thy will', that's when your life begins. What Jesus did was complete love. Until you know the true nature of that love and that it was sent, you won't know how to love.

The Bible also reads in verse 18 that God used love. Verse 18 says *'There is no fear in love, but perfect love casts out fear'.* God used love. Since He is love and since He sent love, He knows that He can now *use* love. When you know the depths and the lengths of what love had to go through to be sent to us, there will be no fear in your heart. Fear begins to disintegrate the closer you are to love. Not man-made love, but God's perfect love casts out fear. Once you know Him and that you yourself cannot remove that fear, you don't have to worry about your insecurities or inadequacies. Those things hurt at times, but when I know that He is love and I know that love was sent, they are removed. When you distance yourself from love, fear arises, but when you are close to that love, faith arises. How far or how close are you? That's why Satan wants to keep you ignorant of God's love. If he keeps you from knowing that love, he will lead you into temptations and traps over and over again. He will use your insecurities against you.

I promise you, if you spend the next 30 + days with God and learn about his love, you will write those books, finish that album, love your mom again, forgive your dad, you will act in love. Do you know the actions of love? As far as what Jesus did, you won't be able to act in love. Because right now whatever you are fearful of is a direct correlation of your distance from love. You have to ask yourself, 'how close am I to God?' If you're close to Him, you will begin to see others clearly.

Verse 19 - 21 reveal how God enables us to love. Verse 19 - 21 says " *But we love because he first loved us. If anyone says I love God and hates his brother, he is a liar for he who does not love his brother whom he has seen cannot love God whom he has not seen. And this commandment we have from him whoever loves God must also love his brother.*" Most of us are not walking in love, we are walking in un-forgiveness, bitterness, and hate. God cannot use a heart with those things in it. Only God can enable us to love and forgive the people who hurt us.

God did not give us a spirit of fear or timidity but a spirit of power, of love and a sound mind (2 Timothy 1:7). This verse is pivotal for your deliverance. Anytime you feel fear, know it originates from your carnal nature or a demonic influence; it doesn't come from God. What come from God is power, love, and a sound mind.

Power

He has first given you a spirit of power. Do you know what kind of power you have? The enemy's objective is to make sure that you don't know how much power you have. He wants to make sure that you are completely blind to the power you have through Christ. Many believers have their hands up as if they are being robbed. Little do they know that they possess the spiritual gun and badge. It would be strange if you walked into a convenience store and an unarmed criminal held up a policeman. Jesus took the keys and the power from Satan. He took the enemy's weapon; the only weapon the enemy has against you is his voice. The moment when Satan talked to Eve in the garden humanity lost its power. He caused Adam and Eve to sacrifice their power and dominion. The only weapon Satan had was his voice. He convinced Adam and Eve to forfeit their dominion. At that moment they gave their power to the enemy. Thankfully, that wasn't the end of the story.

God decided that He would come down on the soil He created and live the life and die the death that we were supposed to. He came to give us the keys and the power. He came to give us the ability to trample over Satan. That's the power we have. Many of us are not walking in that authority and in that power. God has given us a badge and weapon and we are supposed to fight *from* victory, not for victory. When you have the mindset that you are fighting from victory instead of towards victory, you now have all the power you need. The bulk of our warfare is praise and worship. Your voice has power. Through praise, worship, prayer, and fasting you can receive and build up that power.

Love

He also gave you the spirit of love. which is our greatest forms of power. Love has a way of de-escalating things *and* escalating things. Love has a way of de-escalating hate and envy, but also escalating purpose, potentials and aspirations. Love has a way of inspiring, love has a way of helping; God gave us that. When we are in Him and we have His spirit in us, we not only walk with power, we walk with love. One of the main things that we receive from God is a sound mind. If you don't have a sound mind you won't be able to walk in love or use your power. God wants to bring peace to an unstable mind. Fear grows in instability; faith grows with focus. When your mind is sound, focused, and parallel with God's; you are at ease. We were created to be poised - not impulsive. We were created to stand firm - not waver. He gave us that. Anytime you feel fear or insecurity, know that feeling is a direct correlation on how far you are from God. When you know God and you love him and you engage with him every day, fear will no longer torment you. You can be delivered from any soul-ties you have from previous relationships or experiences; you can be freed from the tug of that addiction, you can be freed from that abandonment, you can be freed from what happened to you, but you won't be free until you have been perfected by love. Love has a way of cleansing; love has a way of purging. Today you must let love do it.

A Prayer for freedom

Repeat after me, read this "Father God I receive your love. I repent for allowing fear to run rampant in my life. Father, please allow your love to perfect me; I am tired of being tormented, I am tired of temptations still having a tug. I'm tired of this stronghold in my life. Lord, I need your love to remove these tugs, to remove these ties so that I can walk freely in you. Right now through the authority that has been given to me through Jesus Christ, I speak against every demonic influence, every demonic tie, and every torment. I now walk in the freedom that Christ has given me. I will no longer walk in fear, I will no longer be insecure because I know Who love is, and from now on God, I will stay close. Father, I thank you for your precious spirit; please lead and guide me into all the truth I need to walk away from torment. Thank you Father - I love you. In Jesus' name I do pray. Amen"

COACH JOSH

Singleness is not a particular season; it's seasons. Singleness never ends, because if singleness ends, individuality ends, improvement ends. But since singleness is designed for us to continue to grow, then when I continue to grow I become a better compliment to someone else. Life is about going back and forth from singleness to selflessness. A product is single until it's time to be used. We have to get to a place where we go back and forth from being single and developing to being selfless.

Let's use the analogy of a product. A product is single until it is time to be used. When it's in its container, it is single and whole. From that level of wholeness they now become useful. We have to get to a place in life where we can develop until it is time for us to be used. I know for a fact that as I grow in my singleness, when it is time for me to be used, I can be used properly. The reason why many of us are useless is because we are not selfless. The reason why God cannot use a lot of people in a marriage, business, or in a ministry is because they still have areas they need to improve in. When you know that you are supposed to live life selfless, not selfish, you will have a better chance of staying whole.

You were designed to complement, not to complete.

You were not meant to complete anything; you were meant to complement everything. God is the only one that is capable of completing us; everything else is designed to complement His completion. His completion on the cross and in our lives enables us to complement. Completion is being whole and prepared. Before you complement someone you have to be an original and not a copy. You have to want to be a legend and not a trend. When you are single and allow God to purge you and make you whole, you bring your full self to a relationship and are a perfect complement to your mate. The reason why many of us struggle to make it to the next level in our marriages and careers is because we are not complementing them – we are trying to complete them.

We were designed to complement. The only person that should complete you is Jesus. There is one hole in your heart and there is only One who can fix it: and that's Jesus. We were created to be originals and not copies, legends and not trends and to be significant, not insignificant. Your mate needs the original you. The other person needs your originality. You cannot be an original unless you are connected to the Original, and that's Jesus. When you copy someone else, you're giving that other person someone else, not you.

He also created us to be legendary, not a trend. When you are a trend, you're easily moved, always changing, and never intact. Being legendary is a fruit from being an original. In order for us to be a full for someone else we have to know our significance in Christ. We have to know that all of his children, all of the ones he saved are different because of our significance in him. We have to endeavor to be whole from worship. When we worship God we know our significance in who He is; that's when we become whole. That's when we become more, and more, and more, and more. But when we get so caught up on worshiping our idols, worshiping ourselves, we will miss out on the opportunity to be whole.

Before I conclude this book I want to talk about self-control. God desires for you to have it. In this season, whether single or married, you have to keep this formula in mind: self-denial leads to self-discovery; self-discovery leads to self-development; self-development leads to self-discipline; and self-discipline leads to self-dominance. You have to deny yourself in every season. You have to die to your carnal self and allow God to build your new self. Your old self will always cause you to self-destruct potentially destroying everything connected to you. Scripture addresses this: Before we endeavor to follow Christ we have to deny ourselves, take up our cross and follow Him. In order to completely follow Him through that narrow way, we have to deny our way. Self-denial leads to peace and joy, but when you don't deny yourself, it leads to self-destruction.

Self-denial leads to self-discovery. You discover yourself more when you deny yourself. Life is about discovery - discovering more about God, others, and us. The moment you stop discovering is the moment you begin to deteriorate. In a world that is evolving, you have to evolve. When we deny ourselves we actually discover ourselves. We begin to discover the newness that only comes from being reborn in Christ. When we begin to evolve and grow, we become a living sacrifice. The book of Romans talks about becoming a living sacrifice (12:2), which is our reasonable service. How can we live and die at the same time? That's what we are trying to do every day. As living sacrifices we deny ourselves and let the new self grow. Are you putting your carnal self to death every day? If you don't, that self will grow. Either the regenerated self or the carnal will have your focus. Which one are you focusing on today?

Self-discovery leads to self-development and self-discipline. Momentum builds when you begin to discover more about God, yourself and others. It inspires you to develop and grow. Growth happens in the details and through discipline. If you want to grow, maximize the little things because it's the little foxes that ruin the garden (SOS 2:15). Issues that you leave un-dealt with can spoil your life. Why do you think the Bible talks about little foxes? They come into areas where big foxes can't go. The little foxes begin to eat the vine that grows the fruit. It isn't the big things that destroy you, it's the little things. The big addictions don't destroy you – the small ones do. If you aren't aware of the hidden things that are conceived in your heart, those small things will destroy the big things. If you take the time to address the little details and remain disciplined in the midst of distractions, you will always succeed.

Self-development and self-discipline lead to self-dominance. God told us to have dominance, but before we can have dominion over the things outside of us, we have to have complete dominance on the inside. Are you in control of yourself? Are you completely humbled under the hand of God to teach you how to be in control? God gave us dominion, but we will not be able to have the dominance until we have dominance over ourselves. Are you walking in self-discovery, self-development, self-discipline, self-denial, and self-dominance? If you are not, you're not going to be ready for that next season.

I pray this book was a blessing to you. I pray these worksheets and exercises were a blessing to you. I pray the videos continue to be a blessing to you. And I pray you become more content with where you are. Continue to let God patch those holes in your life and watch overtime you will begin to look like the bucket below.

W1

Reading

Each day carve out no less than 15 minutes to dedicate to reading your Bible. On Monday begin reading Chapters One of the Gospel of John and one chapter each day after that and also begin reading Proverbs Chapter _____ (Whatever day Monday is for you). For example, if next Monday is November 21st began reading Proverbs 21. The goal is to read a proverb a day that matches the day you are on.

Utilize a journal to write down key scriptures that stick out to you and take some time to be still and hear what God may have to say to you about the text. Also, choose a time and a place to dedicate to reading and stay discipline in making sure you meet God every day at that time and place to read and be open to him and his leading.

Meditation

This week we will focus on memorizing 2. Cor 5:17 which says, **17** Therefore, if anyone *is* in Christ, *he is* a new creation; old things have passed away; behold, all things have become new.

Take 5 minutes or so after your daily reading each day to look over this scripture on a notecard and practice it every day until you memorized it and throughout your day when you are attacked with thoughts of who you use to be read this scripture like this out loud "Since I am in Christ I am a new creation my old life and ways have passed away and I will continue to become new"

Prayer and Worship

Check out the prayer plan below and begin to fill out what/ who you will be praying for each day and start Sunday with praying for the week ahead and asking God for favor and wisdom as well as taking some time to reflect on those areas that you could improve on. Remember to follow this formula: **Rejoice Repent**, **Request**, and **Retaliate**. (Aim to spend no less than 15 minutes with God in prayer). You don't have to cram it all in at once you can spend 10 to 15 minutes in the morning and another 10 to 15 minutes at night.

Find a free or paid platform such as Spotify, Pandora, or Apple Music to develop a worship playlist and choose 3 to 7 songs you know for sure connects you quickly to God and into worship. (Remember that true worship is a way of life not just an experience confined within a moment. Use this time to reflect on God and ask him to make you new). Also know that you can utilize this time early in the morning or right when you get up because it's always best to start your day with the one who started your day. Find a quiet place at home or if there is a path near your house take a walk with God with your phone, iPod or MP3 player. Feel free to keep an atmosphere of worship by letting your playlist play periodically while you get dressed preparing for work or your day, while driving or just while resting at home.

Remember Sin separates you from God and in order for God's presence to abide in your home you have to continue to live a **repentant lifestyle**

Relaxation

Choose one or two days this week, if you can, to dedicate 2 hours or more to some form of relaxation/ entertainment whether it is going to see a clean movie, or spend some time hooping (playing basketball) or going to the spa etc. or simply to dedicate that time to nothing but resting and casual activities. Having a day to rest is important it gives you time to detox your spirit soul and body and prepares you for the next week. Remember "If you don't take a Sabbath or a day of rest your health will force you to take one"

List a day you plan to dedicate to rest, relax and reflect.

Accountability and Friendships

On Sunday choose a day in the week to sit down or talk over the phone with a close friend (a friend you can trust) and go over your goals and your plan. After your meeting pick a day each week where the both of you can sit down and go over your or each other's progress depending on whether or not they are a part of this 7-week plan.

Remember accountability is important and without it progress won't be made.

Also remember to choose a person you can trust and if you don't have anyone you can utilize tagging me in any of my social handles and I will make sure to comment. Also ask God to reveal to you who you can confide in.

Recreation and exercise

On Sunday decide which 2 or 3 days you would like to dedicate to exercise. You can choose every other day or multiple days in a row you decide depending on your schedule. This week choose your days and aim to do no less 20 minutes of some sort of exercise per day starting out.

Feel free to utilize free workouts on bodybuilding.com

Week One Worksheet

Sunday Reflection: Goals for the week. | Write down your attainable and sustainable goals for the week. It can be something simple like this week I want to spend 20 minutes in reading and 10 minutes in worship or I want to go get a new membership at a gym. Sunday is your day to reflect and plan for the week. In the box below write down or type in your goals for the week and your accountability partner.

Goals for the week:

Accountability Partner(s):

Reading: Utilize the section below to write down how many minutes did you carve out to read your word, the location and any key scriptures that stood out to you the most. As far as the box at the bottom of this section write down some key things you and your accountability partner talked about during your accountability session.

Day:	Length:	Location:	Key Scripture(s) that stood out to you?
Monday			
Tuesday			
Wednesday			
Thursday			
Friday			
Saturday			

Notes During Accountability Session:

Meditation | Scripture of the week: 2. Cor 5:17 "Therefore, if anyone is in Christ, he is a new creation; old things have passed away; behold, all things have become new"

Reflection: Utilize the section below or your journal to answer the following questions

What does it mean to be in Christ?
What does it mean to be a new creation?
Since you've been in Christ what old things have passed away?
What things in your life currently needs to be made new and what can you do to assist the Holy Spirit to help you make those things new?

Prayer Journal and List: Utilize this page to log in your weekly prayers. Remember prayer changes things. P.U.S.H. Pray Until Something happens and Pray to sustain what happens. | Log your prayer items in the boxes below.

Prayer Formula:			
Rejoice: Before you repent go before God with a thankful heart, letting him know what you are thankful for. The best way to be thankful is to look around you and see what you do have instead of looking ahead.	**Repentance**: Starting your prayers rejoicing reveals to you how great God is and how undeserving you are; leading you to see your heart for what it is which leads you to repentance. Remember repentance is a gift.	**Request**: Once you have rejoiced and repented your request will be in synced with the heart and the will of God and you will begin to ask according to His will!	**Retaliate**: We are in a war and you have the power through Christ over satan and his kingdom. With that being said next you need to retaliate against the enemy and reclaim your dominion. (Warfare prayers are on my site.)
Monday: Focus on Spiritual Disciplines and focus on faith and warfare scriptures. List the areas you need to be disciplined in to the right and use this day to pray for strength. (Warfare scripture will be attached on my website)	Disciplines/ Strengths needed?		
Tuesday: Focus on praying for family and friends. List family friends to the right.	Family and Friends:		
Wednesday: Focus on praying for coworkers and associates also seek God on whom to pray for on this day. Ask people and be open. List those names on the right.	Others:		

UNPLUGGED Thursday: Utilize this day to focus on personal growth (Body Soul and Spirit). Look up scriptures focused on growth and focus on praying on personal growth.	Personal Growth:
Friday: Reflect and seek restoration from the week. Focus on thanksgiving scriptures and Pray thanksgiving prayers focusing on what's around you not ahead of you. List what you are thankful for to the right.	Thankful for:
Saturday: Rest and take some time to pray for your spiritual leaders and for the body of Christ. Pray for revival. List them to the right.	Revival and the Body of Christ:
Sunday: Pray for the week ahead and utilize this day for personal development. Today is a freestyle prayer day list to the right what God wants you to pray for.	God what's on your heart?

Relaxation, Accountability & Exercise: Follow the instructions for each section below

Take some time to answer the questions in each box and utilize the check list below to hold you accountable. Simply write down the first letter (R,A,E) on the day you actually Relaxed, met with accountability partner and exercised.

Relaxation: What days do you plan to relax and what do you plan to do this week to relax?

Accountability: What day(s) do you plan to meet with your accountability partner and what things do you need to cover during your meeting?

Exercise: What days do you plan to work out on and what are your goals for this week? Also what is one thing you need to remove out of your diet?

Monday	Tuesday	Wednesday	Thursday	Friday	Saturday

W2

W2 | Week Two: Lifework Whole Person Plan

Reading

This upcoming Monday start reading chapter 8 in the Gospel of John and make sure to read a Proverb each day.

Journal Writing: Make sure to reflect on each chapter and write down in your journal what stood out to you the most. Never forget reading the Bible without the Author is pointless make sure to pray before reading, asking God to show you what he would like for you to know.

- Tuesday John 8
- Wednesday John 9
- Thursday John 10
- Friday John 11
- Saturday John 12

Utilize a journal or the exercise below to write down key scriptures that stick out to you and take some time to be still and hear what God may have to say to you about the text. Also choose a time and a place to dedicate to reading and stay discipline in making sure you meet God every day at that time and place to read and be open to him and his leading.

Meditation

This week we will focus on memorizing Philippians 4:6-7 [6] do not be anxious about anything, but in everything by prayer and supplication with thanksgiving let your requests be made known to God. [7] And the peace of God, which surpasses all understanding, will guard your hearts and your minds in Christ Jesus.

Take 5 minutes or so after your daily reading each day to look over this scripture on a notecard and practice it every day until you memorized it and throughout your day when you are attacked with thoughts that are against your peace read this scripture like this out loud "Being that I am a daughter/ son of God I will not allow my peace to be taken by worry or fear but I will go immediately to God with all my cares knowing that his peace will guard my mind and heart"

Prayer, Relaxation, Accountability and Recreation

Continue to use the charts below and the directions from week one.

Week Two Worksheet

Sunday Reflection: Goals for the week. | Write down your attainable and sustainable goals for the week.

Goals for the week:
Accountability Partner(s):

Reading: Utilize the section below to write down how many minutes did you carve out to read your word, the location and any key scriptures that stood out to you the most in Proverbs and John.

Day	Length	Location	Key Proverbs that stood out to you?
Monday			
Tuesday			
Wednesday			
Thursday			
Friday			
Saturday			
Other Notes:			

Meditation | Scripture of the week: Philippians 4:6-7 [6] do not be anxious about anything, but in everything by prayer and supplication with thanksgiving let your requests be made known to God. [7] And the peace of God, which surpasses all understanding, will guard your hearts and your minds in Christ Jesus.

Reflection: Utilize the section below or your journal to answer the following questions

Why would worrying be offensive to God?

Why should we take everything both good and bad to God in prayer?

Why do we need God's peace?

In what ways do you worry and how could this scripture help you not to be anxious?

Prayer Journal and List: Utilize this sheet to log in your weekly prayers. Remember prayer changes things. P.U.S.H. Pray Until Something happens and Pray to sustain what happens. | Log your prayer items in the boxes below.

Prayer Formula:			
Rejoice: Before you repent go before God with a thankful heart, letting him know what you are thankful for. The best way to be thankful is to look around you and see what you do have instead of looking ahead.	**Repentance**: Starting your prayers rejoicing reveals to you how great God is and how undeserving you are; leading you to see your heart for what it is which leads you to repentance. Remember repentance is a gift.	**Request**: Once you have rejoiced and repented your request will be in synced with the heart and the will of God and you will begin to ask according to His will!	**Retaliate**: We are in a war and you have the power through Christ over satan and his kingdom. With that being said next you need to retaliate against the enemy and reclaim your dominion. (Warfare prayers are on my site.)
Monday: Focus on Spiritual Disciplines and focus on faith and warfare scriptures. List the areas you need to be disciplined in to the right and use this day to pray for strength. (Warfare scripture will be attached on my website)	Disciplines/ Strengths needed?		
Tuesday: Focus on praying for family and friends. List family friends to the right.	Family and Friends:		
Wednesday: Focus on praying for coworkers and associates also seek God on whom to pray for on this day. Ask people and be open. List those names on the right.	Others:		

UNPLUGGED Thursday: Utilize this day to focus on personal growth (Body Soul and Spirit). Look up scriptures focused on growth and focus on praying on personal growth.	Personal Growth:
Friday: Reflect and seek restoration from the week. Focus on thanksgiving scriptures and Pray thanksgiving prayers focusing on what's around you not ahead of you. List what you are thankful for to the right.	Thankful for:
Saturday: Rest and take some time to pray for your spiritual leaders and for the body of Christ. Pray for revival. List them to the right.	Revival and the Body of Christ:
Sunday: Pray for the week ahead and utilize this day for personal development. Today is a freestyle prayer day list to the right what God wants you to pray for.	God what's on your heart?

Relaxation, Accountability & Exercise: Follow the instructions for each section below

Take some time to answer the questions in each box and utilize the check list below to hold you accountable. Simply write down the first letter (R,A,E) on the day you actually Relaxed, met with accountability partner and exercised.

Relaxation: What days do you plan to relax and what do you plan to do this week to relax?	

Accountability: What day(s) do you plan to meet with your accountability partner and what things do you need to cover during your meeting?

Exercise: What days do you plan to work out on and what are your goals for this week? Also what is one thing you need to remove out of your diet?

Monday	Tuesday	Wednesday	Thursday	Friday	Saturday

W3

W3 |Week Three: Lifework Whole Person Plan

Reading

This upcoming Monday start reading chapter 14 in the Gospel of John and make sure to read a Proverb each day.

Journal Writing: Make sure to reflect on each chapter and write down in your journal what stood out to you the most. Never forget reading the Bible without the Author is pointless make sure to pray before reading asking God to show you what he would like for you to know.

- Monday: John 14
- Tuesday: John 15
- Wednesday: John 16
- Thursday: John 17
- Friday: John 18
- Saturday: John 19

Continue to utilize your journals and reflecting on the main themes in each chapter.

Meditation

This week we will focus on memorizing 1 John 4:18 [18] There is no fear in love, but perfect love casts out fear. For fear has to do with punishment, and whoever fears has not been perfected in love.

Utilize the chart below to help you memorize and to reflect on ways you can overcome fear.

Prayer, Relaxation, Accountability and Recreation

Continue to use the charts below and the directions from week one.

Week Three Worksheet

Sunday Reflection: Goals for the week. | Write down your attainable and sustainable goals for the week.

Goals for the week:
Accountability Partner(s):

Reading: Utilize the section below to write down how many minutes did you carve out to read your word, the location and any key scriptures that stood out to you the most. As far as the box at the bottom of this section write down some key things you and your accountability partner talked about during your accountability session.

Day:	Length:	Location:	Key Scripture(s) that stood out to you?
Monday			
Tuesday			
Wednesday			
Thursday			
Friday			
Saturday			

Other Notes:

Meditation | Scripture of the week: 1 John 4:18 There is no fear in love, but perfect love casts out fear. For fear has to do with punishment, and whoever fears has not been perfected in love.

Reflection: Utilize the section below or your journal to answer the following questions

Why can't our fear and God's love coexist?
How does God's love purge out our fears?
How does fear torment?
In what areas in your life are you tormented by fear and how can you embrace this scripture to help?

Prayer Journal and List: Utilize this sheet to log in your weekly prayers. Remember prayer changes things. P.U.S.H. Pray Until Something happens and Pray to sustain what happens. | Log your prayer items in the boxes below.

Prayer Formula:			
Rejoice: Before you repent go before God with a thankful heart, letting him know what you are thankful for. The best way to be thankful is to look around you and see what you do have instead of looking ahead.	**Repentance**: Starting your prayers rejoicing reveals to you how great God is and how undeserving you are; leading you to see your heart for what it is which leads you to repentance. Remember repentance is a gift.	**Request**: Once you have rejoiced and repented your request will be in synced with the heart and the will of God and you will begin to ask according to His will!	**Retaliate**: We are in a war and you have the power through Christ over satan and his kingdom. With that being said next you need to retaliate against the enemy and reclaim your dominion. (Warfare prayers are on my site.)
Monday: Focus on Spiritual Disciplines and focus on faith and warfare scriptures. List the areas you need to be disciplined in to the right and use this day to pray for strength. (Warfare scripture will be attached on my website)	Disciplines/ Strengths needed?		
Tuesday: Focus on praying for family and friends. List family friends to the right.	Family and Friends:		
Wednesday: Focus on praying for coworkers and associates also seek God on whom to pray for on this day. Ask people and be open. List those names on the right.	Others:		

UNPLUGGED Thursday: Utilize this day to focus on personal growth (Body Soul and Spirit). Look up scriptures focused on growth and focus on praying on personal growth.	Personal Growth:
Friday: Reflect and seek restoration from the week. Focus on thanksgiving scriptures and Pray thanksgiving prayers focusing on what's around you not ahead of you. List what you are thankful for to the right.	Thankful for:
Saturday: Rest and take some time to pray for your spiritual leaders and for the body of Christ. Pray for revival. List them to the right.	Revival and the Body of Christ:
Sunday: Pray for the week ahead and utilize this day for personal development. Today is a freestyle prayer day list to the right what God wants you to pray for.	God what's on your heart?

Relaxation, Accountability & Exercise: Follow the instructions for each section below

Take some time to answer the questions in each box and utilize the check list below to hold you accountable. Simply write down the first letter (R,A,E) on the day you actually Relaxed, met with accountability partner and exercised.

Relaxation: What days do you plan to relax and what do you plan to do this week to relax?	
Accountability: What day(s) do you plan to meet with your accountability partner and what things do you need to cover during your meeting?	
Exercise: What days do you plan to work out on and what are your goals for this week? Also what is one thing you need to remove out of your diet?	

Monday	Tuesday	Wednesday	Thursday	Friday	Saturday

W4

W4 | Week Four: Lifework Whole Person Plan

Reading

This upcoming Monday start reading chapter 20 in the Gospel of John and make sure to read a Proverb each day.

Journal Writing: Make sure to reflect on each chapter and write down in your journal what stood out to you the most. Never forget reading the Bible without the Author is pointless make sure to pray before reading asking God to show you what he would like for you to know.

- Monday: John 20
- Tuesday: John 21
- Wednesday: Luke 1
- Thursday: Luke 2
- Friday: Luke 3
- Saturday: Luke 4

Continue to utilize your journals and reflecting on the main themes in each chapter.

Meditation

This week we will focus on memorizing Philippians 4:13 [13] I can do all things through Christ who strengthens me.

Utilize the chart below to help you memorize and to reflect on ways you can overcome fear.

Prayer, Relaxation, Accountability and Recreation

Continue to use the charts below and the directions from week one.

Week Four Worksheet

Sunday Reflection: Goals for the week. | Write down your attainable and sustainable goals for the week.

Goals for the week:
Accountability Partner(s):

Reading: Utilize the section below to write down how many minutes did you carve out to read your word, the location and any key scriptures that stood out to you the most. As far as the box at the bottom of this section write down some key things you and your accountability partner talked about during your accountability session.

Day:	Length:	Location:	Key Scripture(s) that stood out to you?
Monday			
Tuesday			
Wednesday			
Thursday			
Friday			
Saturday			
Notes During Accountability Session:			

Meditation | Scripture of the week: "Philippians 4:13 [13] I can do all things through Christ who strengthens me."

Reflection: Utilize the section below or your journal to answer the following questions

What are you hear to do? What do you feel your assignment here is?

Why is it important to do everything through Christ?

Why do we need His strength when it comes to our purpose and or our every day life?

In what areas are you weak and need His strength?

Prayer Journal and List: Utilize this sheet to log in your weekly prayers. Remember prayer changes things. P.U.S.H. Pray Until Something happens and Pray to sustain what happens. | Log your prayer items in the boxes below.

Prayer Formula:			
Rejoice: Before you repent go before God with a thankful heart, letting him know what you are thankful for. The best way to be thankful is to look around you and see what you do have instead of looking ahead.	**Repentance**: Starting your prayers rejoicing reveals to you how great God is and how undeserving you are; leading you to see your heart for what it is which leads you to repentance. Remember repentance is a gift.	**Request**: Once you have rejoiced and repented your request will be in synced with the heart and the will of God and you will begin to ask according to His will!	**Retaliate**: We are in a war and you have the power through Christ over satan and his kingdom. With that being said next you need to retaliate against the enemy and reclaim your dominion. (Warfare prayers are on my site.)
Monday: Focus on Spiritual Disciplines and focus on faith and warfare scriptures. List the areas you need to be disciplined in to the right and use this day to pray for strength. (Warfare scripture will be attached on my website)	Disciplines/ Strengths needed?		
Tuesday: Focus on praying for family and friends. List family friends to the right.	Family and Friends:		
Wednesday: Focus on praying for coworkers and associates also seek God on whom to pray for on this day. Ask people and be open. List those names on the right.	Others:		

UNPLUGGED Thursday: Utilize this day to focus on personal growth (Body Soul and Spirit). Look up scriptures focused on growth and focus on praying on personal growth.	Personal Growth:
Friday: Reflect and seek restoration from the week. Focus on thanksgiving scriptures and Pray thanksgiving prayers focusing on what's around you not ahead of you. List what you are thankful for to the right.	Thankful for:
Saturday: Rest and take some time to pray for your spiritual leaders and for the body of Christ. Pray for revival. List them to the right.	Revival and the Body of Christ:
Sunday: Pray for the week ahead and utilize this day for personal development. Today is a freestyle prayer day list to the right what God wants you to pray for.	God what's on your heart?

Relaxation, Accountability & Exercise: Follow the instructions for each section below

Take some time to answer the questions in each box and utilize the check list below to hold you accountable. Simply write down the first letter (R,A,E) on the day you actually Relaxed, met with accountability partner and exercised.

Relaxation: What days do you plan to relax and what do you plan to do this week to relax?					
Accountability: What day(s) do you plan to meet with your accountability partner and what things do you need to cover during your meeting?					
Exercise: What days do you plan to work out on and what are your goals for this week? Also what is one thing you need to remove out of your diet?					

Monday	Tuesday	Wednesday	Thursday	Friday	Saturday

W5

Reading

This upcoming Monday start reading chapter 5 in the Gospel of Luke and make sure to read a Proverb each day.

Journal Writing: Make sure to reflect on each chapter and write down in your journal what stood out to you the most. Never forget reading the Bible without the Author is pointless make sure to pray before reading asking God to show you what he would like for you to know.

- Monday: Luke 5
- Tuesday: Luke 6
- Wednesday: Luke 7
- Thursday: Luke 8
- Friday: Luke 9
- Saturday: Luke 10

Continue to utilize your journals and reflecting on the main themes in each chapter.

Meditation

This week we will focus on memorizing Proverbs 3:5-6 [5] Trust in the Lord with all your heart, and do not lean on your own understanding. [6] In all your ways acknowledge him, and he will make straight your paths.

Utilize the chart below to help you memorize and to reflect on ways you can overcome fear.

Prayer, Relaxation, Accountability and Recreation

Continue to use the charts below and the directions from week one.

Week Five Worksheet

Sunday Reflection: Goals for the week. | Write down your attainable and sustainable goals for the week.

Goals for the week:
Accountability Partner(s):

Reading: Utilize the section below to write down how many minutes did you carve out to read your word, the location and any key scriptures that stood out to you the most. As far as the box at the bottom of this section write down some key things you and your accountability partner talked about during your accountability session.

Day:	Length:	Location:	Key Scripture(s) that stood out to you?
Monday			
Tuesday			
Wednesday			
Thursday			
Friday			
Saturday			
Notes During Accountability Session:			

Meditation | Scripture of the week: Proverbs 3:5-6 [5] Trust in the Lord with all your heart, and do not lean on your own understanding. [6] In all your ways acknowledge him, and he will make straight your paths.

Reflection: Utilize the section below or your journal to answer the following questions

Why is it important to trust God with all of our hearts?

Why can't our understanding be trusted?

Why can God be trusted?

What are those things in your life right now that you find it hard to completely trust God in and why?

Prayer Journal and List: Utilize this sheet to log in your weekly prayers. Remember prayer changes things. P.U.S.H. Pray Until Something happens and Pray to sustain what happens. | Log your prayer items in the boxes below.

Prayer Formula:			
Rejoice: Before you repent go before God with a thankful heart, letting him know what you are thankful for. The best way to be thankful is to look around you and see what you do have instead of looking ahead.	**Repentance**: Starting your prayers rejoicing reveals to you how great God is and how undeserving you are; leading you to see your heart for what it is which leads you to repentance. Remember repentance is a gift.	**Request**: Once you have rejoiced and repented your request will be in synced with the heart and the will of God and you will begin to ask according to His will!	**Retaliate**: We are in a war and you have the power through Christ over satan and his kingdom. With that being said next you need to retaliate against the enemy and reclaim your dominion. (Warfare prayers are on my site.)
Monday: Focus on Spiritual Disciplines and focus on faith and warfare scriptures. List the areas you need to be disciplined in to the right and use this day to pray for strength. (Warfare scripture will be attached on my website)	Disciplines/ Strengths needed?		
Tuesday: Focus on praying for family and friends. List family friends to the right.	Family and Friends:		
Wednesday: Focus on praying for coworkers and associates also seek God on whom to pray for on this day. Ask people and be open. List those names on the right.	Others:		

UNPLUGGED Thursday: Utilize this day to focus on personal growth (Body Soul and Spirit). Look up scriptures focused on growth and focus on praying on personal growth.	Personal Growth:
Friday: Reflect and seek restoration from the week. Focus on thanksgiving scriptures and Pray thanksgiving prayers focusing on what's around you not ahead of you. List what you are thankful for to the right.	Thankful for:
Saturday: Rest and take some time to pray for your spiritual leaders and for the body of Christ. Pray for revival. List them to the right.	Revival and the Body of Christ:
Sunday: Pray for the week ahead and utilize this day for personal development. Today is a freestyle prayer day list to the right what God wants you to pray for.	God what's on your heart?

Relaxation, Accountability & Exercise: Follow the instructions for each section below

Take some time to answer the questions in each box and utilize the check list below to hold you accountable. Simply write down the first letter (R,A,E) on the day you actually Relaxed, met with accountability partner and exercised.

Relaxation: What days do you plan to relax and what do you plan to do this week to relax?
Accountability: What day(s) do you plan to meet with your accountability partner and what things do you need to cover during your meeting?
Exercise: What days do you plan to work out on and what are your goals for this week? Also what is one thing you need to remove out of your diet?

Monday	Tuesday	Wednesday	Thursday	Friday	Saturday

W6

W6 |Week Six: Lifework Whole Person Plan

Reading

This upcoming Monday start reading chapter 11 in the Gospel of Luke and make sure to read a Proverb each day.

Journal Writing: Make sure to reflect on each chapter and write down in your journal what stood out to you the most. Never forget reading the Bible without the Author is pointless make sure to pray before reading asking God to show you what he would like for you to know.

- Monday: Luke 11
- Tuesday: Luke 12
- Wednesday: Luke 13
- Thursday: Luke 14
- Friday: Luke 15
- Saturday: Luke 16

Continue to utilize your journals and reflecting on the main themes in each chapter.

Meditation

This week we will focus on memorizing Hebrews 11:6 [6] And without faith it is impossible to please him, for whoever would draw near to God must believe that he exists and that he rewards those who seek him.

Utilize the chart below to help you memorize and to reflect on ways you can overcome fear.

Prayer, Relaxation, Accountability and Recreation

Continue to use the charts below and the directions from week one.

Week Six Worksheet

Sunday Reflection: Goals for the week. | Write down your attainable and sustainable goals for the week. It can be something simple like this week I want to spend 20 minutes in reading and 10 minutes in worship or I want to go get a new membership at a gym. Sunday is your day to reflect and plan for the week. In the box below write down or type in your goals for the week and your accountability partner.

Goals for the week:
Accountability Partner(s):

Reading: Utilize the section below to write down how many minutes did you carve out to read your word, the location and any key scriptures that stood out to you the most. As far as the box at the bottom of this section write down some key things you and your accountability partner talked about during your accountability session.

Day:	Length:	Location:	Key Scripture(s) that stood out to you?
Monday			
Tuesday			
Wednesday			
Thursday			
Friday			
Saturday			
Other Notes			

Meditation | Scripture of the week: Hebrews 11:6 And without faith it is impossible to please him, for whoever would draw near to God must believe that he exists and that he rewards those who seek him.

Reflection: Utilize the section below or your journal to answer the following questions

Why does it require faith to please God?

Why is it hard for a lot of people to have faith in God?

Why is that before we draw near to God we must know that he exists and that he rewards?

In what areas do you lack faith in God and how could this scripture help?

Prayer Journal and List: Utilize this sheet to log in your weekly prayers. Remember prayer changes things. P.U.S.H. Pray Until Something happens and Pray to sustain what happens. | Log your prayer items in the boxes below.

Prayer Formula:			
Rejoice: Before you repent go before God with a thankful heart, letting him know what you are thankful for. The best way to be thankful is to look around you and see what you do have instead of looking ahead.	**Repentance**: Starting your prayers rejoicing reveals to you how great God is and how undeserving you are; leading you to see your heart for what it is which leads you to repentance. Remember repentance is a gift.	**Request**: Once you have rejoiced and repented your request will be in synced with the heart and the will of God and you will begin to ask according to His will!	**Retaliate**: We are in a war and you have the power through Christ over satan and his kingdom. With that being said next you need to retaliate against the enemy and reclaim your dominion. (Warfare prayers are on my site.)
Monday: Focus on Spiritual Disciplines and focus on faith and warfare scriptures. List the areas you need to be disciplined in to the right and use this day to pray for strength. (Warfare scripture will be attached on my website)	Disciplines/ Strengths needed?		
Tuesday: Focus on praying for family and friends. List family friends to the right.	Family and Friends:		
Wednesday: Focus on praying for coworkers and associates also seek God on whom to pray for on this day. Ask people and be open. List those names on the right.	Others:		

UNPLUGGED Thursday: Utilize this day to focus on personal growth (Body Soul and Spirit). Look up scriptures focused on growth and focus on praying on personal growth.	Personal Growth:
Friday: Reflect and seek restoration from the week. Focus on thanksgiving scriptures and Pray thanksgiving prayers focusing on what's around you not ahead of you. List what you are thankful for to the right.	Thankful for:
Saturday: Rest and take some time to pray for your spiritual leaders and for the body of Christ. Pray for revival. List them to the right.	Revival and the Body of Christ:
Sunday: Pray for the week ahead and utilize this day for personal development. Today is a freestyle prayer day list to the right what God wants you to pray for.	God what's on your heart?

Relaxation, Accountability & Exercise: Follow the instructions for each section below

Take some time to answer the questions in each box and utilize the check list below to hold you accountable. Simply write down the first letter (R,A,E) on the day you actually Relaxed, met with accountability partner and exercised.

Relaxation: What days do you plan to relax and what do you plan to do this week to relax?	
Accountability: What day(s) do you plan to meet with your accountability partner and what things do you need to cover during your meeting?	
Exercise: What days do you plan to work out on and what are your goals for this week? Also what is one thing you need to remove out of your diet?	

Monday	Tuesday	Wednesday	Thursday	Friday	Saturday

W7

W7 | Week Seven: Lifework Whole Person Plan

Reading

This upcoming Monday start reading chapter 17 in the Gospel of Luke and make sure to read a Proverb each day.

Journal Writing: Make sure to reflect on each chapter and write down in your journal what stood out to you the most. Never forget reading the Bible without the Author is pointless make sure to pray before reading asking God to show you what he would like for you to know.

- Monday: Luke 17
- Tuesday: Luke 18
- Wednesday: Luke 19
- Thursday: Luke 20
- Friday: Luke 21
- Saturday: Luke 22

Continue to utilize your journals and reflecting on the main themes in each chapter.

Meditation

This week we will focus on memorizing 2 Timothy 2:4 [4] No soldier gets entangled in civilian pursuits, since his aim is to please the one who enlisted him.

Utilize the chart below to help you memorize and to reflect on ways you can overcome fear.

Prayer, Relaxation, Accountability and Recreation

Continue to use the charts below and the directions from week one.

Week Seven Worksheet

Sunday Reflection: Goals for the week. | Write down your attainable and sustainable goals for the week.

Goals for the week:
Accountability Partner(s):

Reading: Utilize the section below to write down how many minutes did you carve out to read your word, the location and any key scriptures that stood out to you the most. As far as the box at the bottom of this section write down some key things you and your accountability partner talked about during your accountability session.

Day:	Length:	Location:	Key Scripture(s) that stood out to you?
Monday			
Tuesday			
Wednesday			
Thursday			
Friday			
Saturday			
Other Notes			

Meditation | Scripture of the week: 2 Timothy 2:4 [4] No soldier gets entangled in civilian pursuits, since his aim is to please the one who enlisted him.

Reflection: Utilize the section below or your journal to answer the following questions

Why should we as God's Soldiers stay focused on the war at hand?

What are the top things Christians entangle themselves with, keeping them distracted?

What are some things in your life that could be entangling you, keeping you from focusing on your assignment and advancing Gods kingdom?

Prayer Journal and List: Utilize this sheet to log in your weekly prayers. Remember prayer changes things. P.U.S.H. Pray Until Something happens and Pray to sustain what happens. | Log your prayer items in the boxes below.

Prayer Formula:			
Rejoice: Before you repent go before God with a thankful heart, letting him know what you are thankful for. The best way to be thankful is to look around you and see what you do have instead of looking ahead.	**Repentance**: Starting your prayers rejoicing reveals to you how great God is and how undeserving you are; leading you to see your heart for what it is which leads you to repentance. Remember repentance is a gift.	**Request**: Once you have rejoiced and repented your request will be in synced with the heart and the will of God and you will begin to ask according to His will!	**Retaliate**: We are in a war and you have the power through Christ over satan and his kingdom. With that being said next you need to retaliate against the enemy and reclaim your dominion. (Warfare prayers are on my site.)
Monday: Focus on Spiritual Disciplines and focus on faith and warfare scriptures. List the areas you need to be disciplined in to the right and use this day to pray for strength. (Warfare scripture will be attached on my website)	Disciplines/ Strengths needed?		
Tuesday: Focus on praying for family and friends. List family friends to the right.	Family and Friends:		
Wednesday: Focus on praying for coworkers and associates also seek God on whom to pray for on this day. Ask people and be open. List those names on the right.	Others:		

UNPLUGGED Thursday: Utilize this day to focus on personal growth (Body Soul and Spirit). Look up scriptures focused on growth and focus on praying on personal growth.	Personal Growth:
Friday: Reflect and seek restoration from the week. Focus on thanksgiving scriptures and Pray thanksgiving prayers focusing on what's around you not ahead of you. List what you are thankful for to the right.	Thankful for:
Saturday: Rest and take some time to pray for your spiritual leaders and for the body of Christ. Pray for revival. List them to the right.	Revival and the Body of Christ:
Sunday: Pray for the week ahead and utilize this day for personal development. Today is a freestyle prayer day list to the right what God wants you to pray for.	God what's on your heart?

Relaxation, Accountability & Exercise: Follow the instructions for each section below

Take some time to answer the questions in each box and utilize the check list below to hold you accountable. Simply write down the first letter (R,A,E) on the day you actually Relaxed, met with accountability partner and exercised.

Relaxation: What days do you plan to relax and what do you plan to do this week to relax?
Accountability: What day(s) do you plan to meet with your accountability partner and what things do you need to cover during your meeting?
Exercise: What days do you plan to work out on and what are your goals for this week? Also what is one thing you need to remove out of your diet?

Monday	Tuesday	Wednesday	Thursday	Friday	Saturday

COACH JOSH

CPSIA information can be obtained
at www.ICGtesting.com
Printed in the USA
BVHW031826040319
541732BV00001B/68/P